COMMUNICATION THERAPY

for hearing-impaired adults

NORMAN P. ERBER, PH.D.

Clavis Publishing
12 Cook Street
Abbotsford, Victoria 3067
Australia

Copyright © 1988
Clavis Publishing
12 Cook Street
Abbotsford, Victoria 3067
Australia

Cataloging-in-Publication Data

Erber, Norman P.
    Communication therapy for hearing-impaired adults.

    Bibliography
    Includes index
    1. Deaf - Rehabilitation. 2. Audiology.
ISBN 0 7316 3380 6

Printed in Australia
By The Book Printer
Maryborough, Victoria.

CONTENTS

PREFACE

What is *Aural Rehabilitation*? Some audiology students recall a university course with content of dubious value. Many directors of speech and hearing clinics cringe, when they consider a clinical service that's not "cost effective". Numerous hearing-impaired people believe the term is a synonym for "hearing-aid orientation". Most members of the normal-hearing public probably have never heard of it.

During the past fifty years, scientists and engineers have developed a wide range of wearable/insertable electronic hearing aids, increased their electro-acoustic fidelity, and greatly decreased their physical size. These technological advancements are significant and have helped numerous hearing-impaired people receive weak speech sounds and thus communicate more easily. Many adults with acquired hearing losses, however, find that amplification devices do not help them as expected, because their own ears introduce considerable distortion. This perceptual problem is compounded when noise and reverberation obscure the desired speech signal. Moreover, the communication difficulties are not necessarily resolved by lipreading.

Many hearing-impaired people participate in listening or lipreading *courses*, only to learn that they already are maximally using their auditory and visual skills. Some aural rehabilitation specialists are able to provide little more than this type of instruction - a result of the *perceptual* content of many audiology programmes (i.e., with emphasis on hearing tests, hearing aids, hearing rehabilitation, lipreading). In addition, the majority of present-day clinical materials and procedures, derived from laboratory research, tend to be somewhat impractical and unwieldy for serving real people. That is, the activities require too much time, patience, and attention, are too repetitive, and seem unrelated to the needs typically expressed by most clients.

For many years, clinicians have needed a new rehabilitative orientation - an innovative strategy for resolving the communication difficuities that result from hearing loss. The field of aural rehabilitation also has lacked a text that provides students, teachers, and clinicians with a range of practical assessment and therapy procedures, and one that clearly explains how (and why and when) to apply these materials to adults with acquired hearing impairments.

This book is intended to fill some of these long-term needs. Most readers will find it non-technical and easy to follow, although background reading in psycholinguistics, speech science, and aural rehabilitation may clarify the underlying rationale. Chapters on hearing aids, perceptual learning, and counselling are *not* included, as numerous texts already explore those topics in depth (e.g., Hodgson, 1986; Lutman and Haggard, 1983; Erber, 1982, 1985; Cole and Gregory, 1986; Luterman, 1984; Orlans, 1985).

In this book, a new, *conversation-based* approach is proposed for the rehabilitation of adults with acquired hearing loss. **CHAPTER ONE** describes the range of disabilities that can result from acquired hearing impairment and also describes the range of associated "treatments". The hearing clinician's optimal role in the treatment hierarchy is discussed. In **CHAPTER TWO**, a new clinical model for communication therapy is proposed, in which the hearing-impaired person is depicted as the initiator of all verbal interchanges. This non-traditional orientation permits each hearing-impaired client to guide the direction and remediation of conversations. Several new assessment procedures are described in **CHAPTER THREE**. These allow the clinician to quickly estimate the hearing-impaired person's strengths and weaknesses in speech communication. In **CHAPTER FOUR**, numerous clinical activities are suggested, to enhance the client's conversation-management skills. These incorporate problem-identification and problem-solving components, to help the client avoid difficulty and resolve communication breakdown. A combined auditory-visual approach to communication therapy is promoted. Language-use strategies are emphasized, rather than increased reliance on impaired perceptual abilities. In **CHAPTER FIVE**, electronic hearing-loss simulation is introduced as an efficient means for counselling and instructing friends and family members in speech and language clarification. Detailed examples are provided. Persistent clinical needs and directions for applied research in numerous areas are considered in **CHAPTER SIX**.

The methods described in this text were formulated primarily to motivate and inspire our hearing-impaired clients and their student clinicians. The traditional approach - perceptual assessment and practice - obviously was limited in usefulness. Friendship and social interaction were not considered to be sufficient reasons for maintaining the weekly clinics. The hearing-impaired adults desired interesting materials and relevant procedures to assist them in daily conversation; the student clinicians desired theoretical consistency and clinical practicality. We needed a new approach to the rehabilitation of hearing-impaired adults. So, I loaded some provisions into Old Paint - my boomerangs, my old typewriter, a carton of Kit Kats, and a supply of Swan Lager - and headed into the Outback once again.....

The contents of this book, therefore, are somewhat personal. I lived it, wrote it, re-wrote it, drew all the figures and diagrams, and typeset the text (i.e., blame *me*). I also annoyed fellow staff members by monopolizing the department's Apple Macintosh word processor (for several years!). Sorry - Jan, Jennie, Paul, and Margaret. I was obsessed.

Finally, my sincere thanks to graphic masters Michael Veldman and John Farrell, who patiently demonstrated keyboard skills, and to several colleagues who examined previous drafts of the manuscript: Louise Brown, Brad Edgerton, Susan Goldie, Susan Inglis, and Allen Montgomery. They gleefully pointed out my typographical errors, incoherent sentences, and lapses of logic. I helped them feel proudly literate.

Norman P. Erber, Ph.D.
Senior Lecturer - Department of Communication Disorders
Lincoln School of Health Sciences/LaTrobe University
625 Swanston Street
Carlton, Victoria 3053 Australia

HEARING DISABILITIES AND TREATMENTS

METHODS OF AURAL REHABILITATION

The clinical specialty of Aural Rehabilitation was formed in the late 1940s, when professionals in the newly established field of Audiology turned their attention to the communication problems of the returning servicemen and women of World War II. Many of these disabled individuals had suffered serious hearing losses, as the result of noise exposure or head injury.

At that time, three major aural rehabilitation tools were available to the clinician: hearing aids, auditory training, and lipreading instruction. The electrical *hearing aids* of that period were relatively large, heavy, and uncomfortable. It could be shown, however, that these devices provided useful speech information at high sound levels to deafened individuals, and that they successfully helped overcome large losses of hearing sensitivity. The *auditory training* procedures had been derived from early hearing-education programmes of Urbantschitsch (1895) and Goldstein (1939). These organized frameworks for teaching provided models for the mainly analytical listening exercises which were created and applied to help individuals re-learn listening skills (see Carhart, 1961). A wide range of specialized *lipreading-instruction* procedures and practice materials also had been in use for many years. Because most of these visual-perception techniques were developed before the era of effective electrical hearing aids, lipreading often was practised without associated acoustic cues for speech. Some methods of lipreading instruction encouraged careful attention to the speaker's visible articulations. Others stressed the use of all available linguistic cues for interpretation of spoken messages (see Jeffers and Barley, 1971; Berger, 1972).

Nearly all communication therapists continue to apply these three basic, traditional components of aural rehabilitation. Most clinicians, however, now give their greatest emphasis to *hearing aid selection and adjustment* (see Hodgson, 1986), and they direct less of their attention to development of the person's listening or lipreading skills. This trend is mainly the result of extensive improvements in hearing aid design and construction during the past 40 years, leading to greatly increased fidelity of electroacoustic sound reproduction (Studebaker and Bess, 1982; Byrne, 1986).

There is another reason, however, for the recent ascendency of hearing aids as therapeutic tools: aural rehabilitation specialists appear to have lost confidence in both auditory training and lipreading instruction as effective rehabilitation techniques. They continue to recognize that hearing-impaired people need to learn to use their (aided) hearing effectively, and that these individuals also must maximize their use of complementary visible cues to perceive speech most accurately. Many clinicians, however, doubt that concentrated listening and lipreading instruction (at least as traditionally practised) have significant long-term effects on a hearing-impaired person's success in daily verbal communication, and some research tends to support that view (Binnie, 1977; Lundborg, Risberg, Holmqvist, Lindstrom, and Svard, 1982; Lesner, Sandridge, and Kricos, 1987).

This situation is complicated by a growing feeling among professionals that particular aspects of *all* these apparently well-established clinical procedures are seriously deficient. For example, many hearing-impaired people express dissatisfaction with their hearing aids, claiming that even well designed and constructed, modern amplification devices are inadequate for their auditory requirements*. Others show little improvement after a well-organized sequence of stepped auditory training lessons. Some hearing-impaired people simply lose interest and do not return to attend all sessions of a course in lipreading. Even when discussion sessions are organized, where hearing-impaired adults can compare their own experiences, communication difficulties, and personal solutions, many commonly reported difficulties are not resolved, and a sense of frustration, isolation, a lack of satisfying social contact, or an absence of empathy from friends and relatives may remain.

In response to these acknowledged shortcomings of the older and more traditional methods, a newer and more "progressive" approach to aural rehabilitation has been proposed (McCarthy and Alpiner, 1982). In this supplement to the more traditional therapies, various new techniques are introduced for use, typically in small therapy groups. Sessions may be devoted to applying problem-solving techniques, developing "coping" strategies, learning assertiveness and tactics for optimizing the communication process, and achieving personal adjustment (see Kaplan, 1982). In short, clinicians have begun to employ a variety of counselling methods to help hearing-impaired adults overcome or adapt to many of the difficulties that result from a loss of those hearing abilities which previously had permitted normal human interaction.

Some clinicians are beginning to recognize that the "progressive" approach to aural rehabilitation is partly a response to their own frustration

---

* Many hearing-impaired people who apparently *need* hearing aids do not obtain them or use them (Franks and Beckmann, 1985). Their "needs", however, usually are established according to the clinician's audiometric results, which may differ from the client's personal criteria. Most hearing-impaired people tend to want increased speech *clarity*, but present-day hearing aids deliver mainly increased speech *intensity*. The result is amplified speech that is audible, but which still is perceived without clarity.

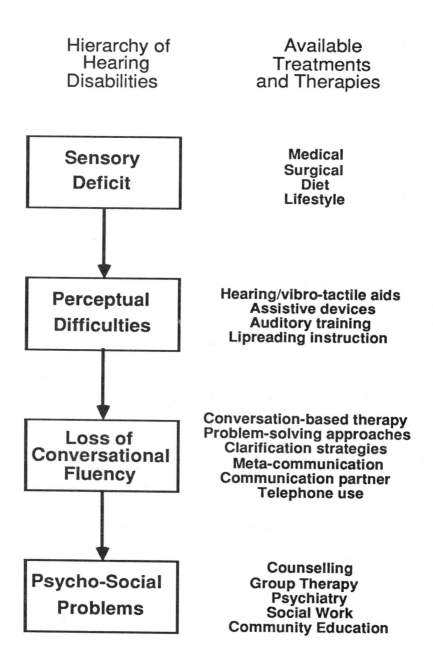

Figure 1-1. Hierarchy of hearing disabilities and their treatments.

- which can result when the more traditional aural rehabilitation therapies fail to satisfy the needs of hearing-impaired clients. As a consequence, clinicians may choose to alter (usually diminish) their clients' expectations for restored auditory function and verbal communication, and to promote the use of alternative "coping" strategies instead.

Another developing point of view (Pengilley, 1977) suggests that a client's overall communication difficulties result not only from his/her hearing disability but *also* from the failure of communication partners to understand the nature of hearing impairment and to assist in a positive manner. It is proposed that society share responsibility with the hearing-impaired person for minimizing any communication difficulties. Thus community-education programmes are established and are directed to informing and guiding all members of the public to enhance their verbal communication with hearing-impaired people - at least cooperating fully when they receive requests for clarification during daily conversation.

Each philosophy and clinical activity contains beneficial components which can make communication easier for hearing-impaired people. There still is much to do, however, if we wish to develop a comprehensive rehabilitation programme which satisfies clients, clinicians, and the communicating public.

HIERARCHY OF DISABILITIES

In general, communication therapists gain most of their professional and personal satisfaction from helping hearing-impaired people communicate more easily. To be consistently rewarding, the results of therapy must be apparent in ways that both clinicians and their clients can clearly recognize. In short, to reach our own goals, we must help our clients reach *theirs*. The first step in the process is to appreciate the nature of hearing impairment and its wide-ranging effects on an individual. That is, we need to describe the many ways that deterioration in or damage to a person's auditory system can lead to complex human discomforts, disabilities, and even handicaps. Then we can begin to devise a set of rehabilitation strategies.

Conductive/Sensory Loss

Hearing loss and its consequences can be described on many different levels (Corso, 1977; World Health Organization, 1980) (Figure 1-1). For example, from one point of view, hearing loss is characterized simply by reference to the *anatomical* and *physiological* changes that occur in one's ears (Figure 1-2). That is, a conductive or sensorineural loss is made evident through the presence of modified, damaged, or missing anatomical structures in the auditory system (e.g., hair cells or auditory nerve fibres). This disruption may make the hearing mechanism less sensitive to weak sounds, less frequency-discriminative, less accurate in time resolution, and so forth (Bailey, 1983; Evans, 1983). As a result, the ear delivers altered patterns of nerve impulses to the auditory processing and association areas of the brain.

Perceptual Loss

If this altered sensory information is modified sufficiently (relative to the normal patterns previously received), the consequence quite often is a *perceptual* dysfunction, in which the detection, discrimination, and/or identification of incoming sound patterns (via their neural correlates) is disturbed, if not significantly distorted (Sanders, 1982; Erber, 1982; Bailey, 1983). Moreover, if the peripheral structures of the auditory system are altered too greatly, then even the *potential* for satisfactory auditory perception may be greatly diminished (see Plomp, 1978; Byrne, 1986). For example, two different incoming sound signals (e.g., the words *feet* and *soup*) may trigger essentially the same coded neural pattern, and thus they may be virtually indistinguishable to the listener (Table 1-1). If so, the individual may learn to rely on input from *other* sensory systems to compensate for this loss of discriminative auditory information. For example, a hearing-impaired person may become very dependent on *vision* as an aid to differentiation and thus identification of a speaker's utterances. From one point of view, we may consider this increased reliance on visual cues during verbal interaction to represent "atypical" perceptual processing - at least in relation to the individual's former (mainly auditory) method of perceiving spoken language.

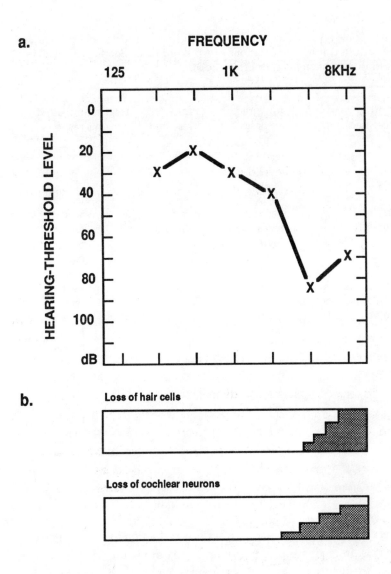

Figure 1-2. Impaired hearing, described in terms of: (a) audiometric responses to pure tones; and (b) the condition of anatomical structures in the inner ear (after Schucknecht, 1974).

Table 1-1. Some typical auditory word-identification errors made by hearing-impaired adults during presentations of AB Word Lists (Boothroyd, 1968) in a quiet testing environment (after Erber, 1985).

Word presented		Hearing-impaired person's response	Word presented		Hearing-impaired person's response
fan	>	sand	heel	>	feel
both	>	boat	shop	>	chop
cheek	>	chick	vet	>	bet
jot	>	yacht	weep	>	wheat
cheese	>	she's	sack	>	tack
hive	>	high	fill	>	feel
moss	>	moth	catch	>	cat
thud	>	mud	thumb	>	sum
wrap	>	rat	heap	>	heat
vice	>	bike	wise	>	wine
shown	>	show	rave	>	rays
bomb	>	bob	hutch	>	hut
will	>	wheel	kill	>	till
vat	>	bat	thighs	>	fives
wreath	>	reef	wave	>	way
guess	>	guest	reap	>	rip
comb	>	cone	foam	>	phone
choose	>	shoes	goose	>	booth
sum	>	fun	reach	>	rich

Interactive Loss

A perceptual loss can result in a serious reduction in sound *appreciation*, that is, in enjoyment of previously pleasant sound qualities. For example, the hearing-impaired person may no longer be able to derive pleasure from the sounds of music, birds singing, or the human voice, perhaps because of the low audibility of these sounds or because of distortions in their sound qualities. The hearing-impaired individual also may have lost the pleasure of listening to speech via the radio, television, or film, because of the great effort that is required to understand what people are saying.

Most hearing-impaired people with perceptual disabilities also experience some difficulty in person-to-person, *interactive* communication (Table 1-2). They may notice that these communication problems occur under a variety of conditions: for example, during an acoustic-only conversation, as over the telephone; during a predominantly visual conversation, as in a very noisy room; or in extreme cases, they may even encounter repeated conversational breakdowns during ordinary face-to-face dialogue in a quiet environment.

The hearing-impaired person may consider these conversational deviations to be very disruptive to daily life. The individual may feel that most time is spent *not* in exchanging desired information, opinions, or feelings, but in "repairing" conversations when misunderstandings occur. The degree of discomfort that results will vary considerably according to the hearing-impaired individual's personality* and desire for social contact, as well as his/her dependency on verbal communication for maintenance of friendships, professional relationships, and job satisfaction.

Psycho-Social Loss

These interruptions in the ease and fluency of personal interactions - both with the surrounding social environment as well as with regular communication partners - can affect the hearing-impaired person's overall feeling of well-being (see Kaplan, 1982; Kyle, 1985; Meadow-Orlans, 1985). If he/she is seriously disturbed by the loss of consistency in verbal-acoustic interactions, the hearing-impaired individual may gradually develop mild or even serious psychological symptoms such as

---

* An individual's linguistic abilities, personal interests, self-confidence, motivation, and persistence all determine the effects of hearing loss on one's communicative behaviour and lifestyle.

Table 1-2. Some difficulties that often occur in conversations between hearing-impaired people and their communication partners.

---

1. Turn-taking rituals may be disrupted (e.g., the hearing-impaired person may not respond when cued; silent intervals or interruptions may occur; the hearing-impaired person may dominate the conversation).

2. The hearing person may begin to compensate for or adapt to the communication style of the hearing-impaired person - i.e., may attempt to make communication easier by consciously modifying vocabulary or language to match that of the hearing-impaired person.

3. The hearing person may introduce awkward intervals by consciously planning utterances for presumed high intelligibility.

4. The hearing person may slow his/her overall rate of speech, may increase intensity, or may exaggerate prosody and articulation while attempting to make communication easier for the hearing-impaired person.

5. Either communicator may use non-verbal cues excessively to clarify intent or content. Gesture, posture, eye contact, and/or facial expressions may be emphasized or exaggerated.

6. As the result of misperceptions (and thus misdirections), the hearing-impaired communicator may unintentionally introduce a new topic.

7. Topics may be intentionally avoided or discontinued, if either communicator judges them to contain vocabulary or language that consistently create perceptual difficulties for the hearing-impaired person.

---

irritability, anxiety, depression, neurosis, or paranoia (Rousey, 1976), as well as an extreme sense of isolation and powerlessness (Schlesinger, 1985).

Thus, we see that a hierarchy (progression) of disability can emerge from the deficit imposed by a conductive and/or sensorineural hearing loss. If appropriate intervention or treatment is not applied early, serious

Table 1-2. continued

---

8. The hearing person may begin to communicate more superficially than is typical with others - in reaction to repeated clarification requests made by the hearing-impaired person, or as the result of continued confusion.

9. Both communicators may frequently engage in diversions (side issues) to clarify confusions, thereby diminishing the fluency of the conversation.

10. Both communicators may become conscious of the abnormality/difficulty of the conversation, and begin to discuss *that* as a topic. As a result, entire conversations may be composed of meta-communication.

11. Both communicators may avoid attempting to express intimacy, strong feelings, or highly emotional experiences, given the difficulty of conveying such subtle aspects of an utterance (e.g., irony and sarcasm depend on syllable duration, voice pitch, prosody, and voice quality). This may affect development of a close, long-term relationship between the communicators.

12. Either communicator may (pretend to) be satisfied with incomplete understanding during the conversation.

13. Either communicator may intentionally shorten conversations - to minimize or end frustration, stress, or communication difficulty.

---

symptoms may develop at several levels of human function, occasionally with overwhelming consequences.

HIERARCHY OF TREATMENTS

What sort of treatments or therapies can be applied to avert, or at least minimize, the potentially disabling or handicapping effects of hearing loss? Specialists treat the disorder in as many different ways as there are different levels of disability. Each remedial approach tends to be directed to a specific level in the disability hierarchy (Figure 1-1).

Medical/Surgical Treatment or Intervention

Many ear, nose, and throat specialists tend to recognize hearing loss primarily as an anatomical/physiological abnormality, and so they are oriented toward treating the sensory deficit *itself*. For example, if the hearing problem has resulted from a blockage or stiffness in the outer or middle ear, medical or surgical treatment is a routine choice. Medication and/or prosthetic surgery can be quite effective in restoring the conductive pathway for incoming sound (see Beagley, 1981).

If tinnitus is the major complaint, then stress relief, medication, relaxation therapy, or (acoustic) distraction may reduce the symptoms (Bentler and Tyler, 1987; Slater, 1987). In general, however, cochlear hearing disorders in which there is significant hair-cell damage or loss have not been successfully treated either medically or surgically.

Yet, we note that in recent years, surgeons have been able to provide/restore some auditory sensation to profoundly deaf people (Owens, 1983; Eisenberg, 1985; Schindler and Merzenich, 1985). The cochlear implant systems have included single stimulators or arrays of tiny electrodes, activated by sophisticated electronic speech-signal processing systems. Many cochlear prostheses have been implanted - in children as well as in adults. The benefits that individuals derive from cochlear implantation range from gross sound awareness to good understanding of conversational speech (typically with the use of limited visual cues). Important factors relating to communication success seem to be: the age of the patient; etiology of the hearing loss; auditory nerve function; the number of years without hearing; the type of pre-implant counselling; the type of post-implant instruction; and the configuration of the cochlear implant device.

Perceptual Enhancement

A sensory deficit, if serious enough or left untreated, usually becomes apparent as a perceptual disorder. This means that the affected individual will begin to encode, process, and store incoming speech signals in short-term memory in ways that are different from normal, and that presumably are less efficient. For example, the hearing-impaired person may hear two distinctive speech elements (which in fact, do sound different to someone with normal hearing) as having essentially the same acoustic quality. For example, specific pairs of speech sounds such as /b,d/, /f,θ/, or /m,n/ will appear to be very similar (Walden, Montgomery, Prosek, and Schwartz, 1980). The listener may begin to assign both members of a pair the same verbal label (e.g., /b/, /f/, or /m/, respectively), or may begin to respond randomly (e.g., /b/ or /d/, /f/ or /θ/, /m/ or /n/). These error tendencies are likely to be magnified if speech is presented at a rapid rate, producing numerous word and sentence misperceptions as well.

Throughout the history of aural rehabilitation as a therapeutic process, most of our clinical efforts have been applied at the level of *perception*. That is, we have expended most of our professional energy in attempts to eliminate or at least minimize the *perceptual* effects of hearing loss. This choice of emphasis is understandable, as most of the research into hearing loss and hearing rehabilitation has been the product of *audiologists* - who have tended to describe hearing disabilities primarily in *perceptual* terms.

Hearing aids

One of the audiologist's principal rehabilitative tools is the electronic hearing aid. Given the availability of such devices, clinicians usually recommend hearing aids to most hearing-impaired individuals who exhibit sensitivity losses, that is, those who have difficulty detecting sounds. Because hearing aids primarily *amplify* sound, these devices can assist most people whose major auditory difficulty is a loss of *sensitivity* to weak sounds, and they can even help many whose ears *distort* audible sounds. Over the years, electronic designers have created hearing aids in various configurations to help hearing-impaired people with specific auditory needs: e.g., binaural aids, CROS aids, all-in-the-ear aids, those with automatic gain control, directional microphones, wireless microphone-transmitters, and so forth (Hodgson, 1986).

Assistive amplification devices

In addition to the more conventional hearing aids mentioned above (e.g., those worn behind or in the ear), a wide range of amplification devices for specific applications are now available to assist hearing-impaired people. These supplementary amplifiers and/or adapters make listening easier when one uses the telephone, watches television, attends meetings, or listens in the theatre (Hurvitz and Carmen, 1981; Hodgson, 1986). In some instances, sound signals are detected and transmitted from the source to the hearing-impaired person via long wires, induction loops, radio waves, or infra-red radiation. In other applications (e.g., to assist listening over the telephone), the output speech signal is *transduced* (e.g., to electro-magnetic form) for more efficient listening - via a hearing aid set to the "T" position. In general, these various devices make the sounds delivered to the listener's ear louder than they would otherwise be.

Tactile aids

In some hearing-impaired individuals, the auditory sensory mechanism, the organ of Corti, has not developed normally or has been destroyed due to drugs, trauma, or disease. All that remains is *vibro-tactile* sensation - extreme sensitivity losses suggested by "corner audiograms". In these cases, to restore or develop perceptual function, the audiologist may recommend a *vibro-tactile* aid (see DeFilippo, 1982b; Plant, Macrae, Dillon, and Pentecost, 1984).

Several tactile speech-perception aids are available at present. Some of these are portable, and consist of a small battery-powered unit which contains a microphone and amplifier, and which is connected to the tactile transducer(s) by a fine wire (Lubinsky, 1983; Plant, Macrae, Dillon, and Pentecost, 1984). Other tactile aids are larger and are used mainly for instruction in speech production and perception in a clinic or school (Schulte, 1978). In either case, the tactile cues are received through the wrist, fingertips, chest, or another part of the body.

Typically, a profoundly hearing-impaired person can easily perceive speech-intensity patterns through any of the available devices. In some experimental units, frequency-selective information also is made available - by means of a "speech processor", which delivers spectral cues in the form of *place* differences (e.g., different fingers) or *quality* differences (e.g., rough/smooth or punctate/diffuse sensations at the same place) (see Pickett, 1979; DeFilippo, 1982b; Roeser, Friel-Patti, and Henderson, 1983; Blamey and Clark, 1987; Weisenberger and Miller, 1987). All these tactile devices provide useful sensory information to assist lipreaders, which certainly is much better than acoustic isolation (McCall, 1984). None of them, however, is yet an adequate substitute for the lost hearing of the profoundly deaf.

Listening / auditory learning

Auditory learning is a process by which the hearing-impaired person develops his/her perceptual skills through guided listening practice (see Erber, 1982, 1985; Sanders, 1982; Cole and Gregory, 1986). In the course of therapy, the clinician may help the hearing-impaired client: (1) to exploit all available auditory information during (auditory-visual) speech perception; (2) to participate more effectively in conversations where only *acoustic* information is available (e.g., over the telephone); (3) to recognize acoustic cues made newly available by recently acquired hearing aids; and/or (4) to recognize the perceptual limitations of one's own auditory system.

Assessment generally involves describing the hearing-impaired person's auditory vowel and consonant confusions, as well as auditory word/sentence perception and conversational fluency. Listening practice may reflect the range of stimulus-response tasks shown in Figure 1-3 (Erber; 1982). During practice sessions, an "Adaptive Communication" approach often is used. For example, following *successes* with a particular combination of stimulus and response (e.g., sentence identification), the clinician will present more challenging practice activities (e.g., sentence comprehension). *Difficulties* lead to remedial work with simpler stimulus-response tasks (e.g., phrase discrimination).

STIMULUS

RESPONSE	Speech unit	Syllable	Word	Phrase	Sentence	Narrative
Detection						
Discrimination						
Identification						
Comprehension						

Figure 1-3. A stimulus-response matrix. The clinician selects each communication task on the basis of the client's degree of success with those which have preceded it (after Erber, 1982).

Listening practice usually takes place under conditions where *visual* cues for speech are intentionally limited. For example, the clinician may obscure the mouth with a hand or card while speaking, may look down or turn the head, may speak while sitting behind or beside the client, or may present *recorded* materials for listening practice. These auditory-only conditions are easily interspersed with auditory-visual communication. To require *listening*, the clinician simply obscures the mouth. Telephone communication, a common auditory-only task, may be introduced as well - to provide practical, everyday listening experiences (see Erber, 1985).

Lipreading

In cases where amplification devices and careful listening do not completely restore functional auditory perception, the hearing-impaired person usually turns to another sensory system - vision - to compensate for the missing acoustic information. The application of didactic approaches to lipreading instruction dates back to the early 1900s (see reviews by Jeffers and Barley, 1971; Berger, 1972). In some of the methods (which continue to be employed effectively), the instructor helps the hearing-impaired person learn to discriminate and/or identify the range of mouth shapes that visually convey spoken linguistic information (see Walden, Erdman, Montgomery, Schwartz, and Prosek,1981). Photos, videotape, or live presentation may be used as media. Practice may be conducted silently (i.e., without voice), with vocal cues, or in the presence of background noise to partly mask the acoustic speech stimuli.

Other approaches guide the hearing-impaired lipreader to make effective "guesses" about the content of sentences. The client learns to base these hypotheses on those portions of the spoken utterance that are received with greater confidence, on redundancies in the message, and on known linguistic rules (Hull,1976). Attention is directed to situational, contextual, and/or gestural cues as well - to supplement available oral/facial information (Berger and Popelka, 1971; Garstecki and O'Neill, 1980).

Many lipreading-instruction techniques were developed before the advent of effective hearing aids, and so they are mainly procedures for enhancing *silent* visual perception of speech. More recently, however, several methods that employ sentences and connected discourse have been developed to assist hearing-impaired people blend visual input with the minimal complementary acoustic (or tactile) cues that they concurrently receive (DeFilippo and Scott, 1978; Garstecki, 1981a; Owens and Telleen, 1981; Montgomery, Walden, Schwartz, and Prosek, 1984).

Conversation Conservation

If the hearing-impaired individual experiences significant perceptual difficulty, and if the problem affects his/her communication activities for an extended time, then the quality of that person's interactions with people in the surrounding environment is likely to deteriorate. A variety of interactive *communication therapies* has evolved in recent years. The intent of all these approaches is to help people avoid or overcome any disabilities that result from a change in natural interaction with others.

As most human interactions tend to take the form of *conversations*, various conversation-based therapies have been devised specifically to help hearing-impaired people resolve conversational disfluency or breakdown. Some of these involve the application of: partial scripts; contingent pairs; QUEST?AR; ASQUE>>>; role playing; TOPICON; problem-solving; and clarification strategies - all described in later sections of this book.

These various approaches include techniques for anticipating and/or avoiding communication difficulty as well as preparing for various conversational formats, contents, and message types. Practice includes examining and discussing probable directions that a conversation may follow, as well as anticipating likely questions and answers. The clinician also may help the hearing-impaired client develop a set of problem-solving skills: how to recognize that a communication problem has occurred; how to specify the source of the communication breakdown; how to apply various clarification and repair strategies; how to request assistance from the other (normal-hearing) communicator; and how to judge the appropriateness of the applied or requested strategy and evaluate its success. Many of these approaches already have been incorporated into a clinical telephone-communication programme for hearing-impaired people (Erber, 1985).

Because all conversations are carried out between at least two people, it is important to extend our rehabilitative efforts beyond the hearing-impaired person him/herself. That is, we often can help the client more effectively by *dividing* our professional attention, and devoting a share of our effort to instructing and/or counselling family members and close friends (Clezy, 1979, 1984; Webster and Newhoff, 1981). For example, we can explain and demonstrate the nature of hearing impairment, we can show how this affects speech communication, and we can help the normal-hearing relative or friend make major contributions to conversational fluency (see Chapter 5).

Community education programmes* are similar in overall purpose, but are much broader in scope. In this instance, we try to provide the same type of information to a large number of (normal-hearing) people who do not necessarily need the information *at that moment*. The primary aims are to raise the level of awareness of the general public, to make them conscious of the numerous hearing-impaired people who live among them in the community, and to prepare them for those rare(?) occasions when they find themselves in a conversation with a hearing-impaired person**.

Psycho-Social Therapy

If the hearing-impaired person's interactive difficulties are allowed to progress, serious breakdowns in conversation may repeatedly occur. Depending on the individual, these disruptions may lead to feelings of powerlessness, frustration, anger, self-pity, suppressed aggression, and/or withdrawal from social interaction with family and friends (Eriksson-Mangold and Erlandsson, 1984; Schlesinger, 1985). A psychologist, social worker, counsellor, or psychiatrist may be required to help the hearing-impaired person re-establish meaningful and satisfying social contact (Rook, 1984; Kyle, Jones, and Wood, 1985). Achieving

---

* Community education also is often required in special contexts, such as in geriatric hospitals and in nursing homes. In these centres, all staff members regularly interact with hearing-impaired patients, so they all must learn techniques for achieving conversational fluency (Hull, 1982).

** This approach to education is similar to that used to train police, fire, and paramedical personnel to deal with those who are blind or physically disabled and also to prepare the general public for natural disasters, by means of fire drills and first aid, cardio-pulmonary resuscitation, and water life-saving courses.

these objectives may require a specially trained and experienced psycho-therapist or social worker - one who is familiar with the potentially serious problems that can result from a hearing loss that has not been effectively treated as a sensory, perceptual, or interactive disorder (Lieth, 1972b). This therapeutic work may need to be carried out in consultation with other professionals, such as an audiologist, speech-language pathologist, or otolaryngologist.

CHOICE OF THERAPEUTIC LEVEL

The Client's Needs and Goals

Most hearing-impaired adults who attend our clinics for communication therapy have known for several years that their hearing ability has been gradually diminishing. For example, some people realize that they cannot detect the sounds of *weak* fricative consonants (e.g., /f/ and /θ/), or even confuse particular voiced sounds that are quite *audible* (e.g., /m/ and /n/). They may be aware that they are unable to understand specific voices over the telephone, or cannot receive speech clearly in group discussions or in other noisy places. They may report communication difficulties at work; they may feel excluded from family group activities; or they may intentionally avoid contact with former friends. Other hearing-impaired people, however, cannot specify so precisely what is making them uncomfortable or unhappy, but they do recognize that they have considerable difficulty understanding speech when people talk to them, and thus they are unable to communicate fluently during conversations.

During a case-history interview, or while completing a questionnaire, many of our hearing-impaired clients will state that their principal goal is to be able to communicate easily again. Usually, they suggest that this is the main reason that they want to learn to lipread or want to try using hearing aids. That is, many hearing-impaired adults consider their main problem to be a loss of *conversational fluency*, and they want to overcome this interactive disability (Stephens, 1980). Previously, when they had normal hearing, they could easily listen for detail, comment with subtlety, or confidently express a well-developed sense of humour. Now that they are hearing impaired, they may have great difficulty applying their previous conversational styles to achieve their current communication goals. These goals may include: establishing or continuing friendships; expressing warmth and human understanding; obtaining or providing information; discussing interesting topics; acquiring or maintaining status, influence, or control; and so forth. This change in one's interpersonal style, verbal power, and social status can significantly affect one's self confidence and can lead to serious psychological dilemmas. Restoration of conversational fluency, therefore, has become one of our main clinical objectives.

The Clinician's Skills

The effect of some forms of hearing impairment, such as otosclerosis, can be successfully treated medically or surgically. At the other extreme, some hearing-impaired individuals (as well as their families) may have devloped serious psycho-social problems, which require the attention of a skilled counsellor or therapist. We ordinarily refer hearing-impaired clients in either group to appropriate health-care specialists, maintaining contact as consultants where necessary.

Most hearing-impaired adults who attend our clinics, however, do not fit into either of these categories. They need neither medical, surgical, nor extensive psycho-therapeutic help. Instead, their reported problems are either *perceptual* and/or *conversational* (interactive) in nature. What can we offer them? How can we optimally provide communication therapy to these hearing-impaired people?

Let us consider the special knowledge and skills that we clinicians* possess. To summarize our professional competence in this area: (1) we understand the effects of hearing loss on perception of speech and on human interaction; (2) we are familiar with numerous traditional approaches to aural rehabilitation, such as auditory evaluation, hearing aid

---

* Speech-language pathologists, teachers of hearing-impaired children, audiologists, and so forth.

selection and orientation, speech-perception testing, auditory training, lipreading evaluation and instruction, as well as basic aspects of counselling; (3) we possess general backgrounds in language form and function, with knowledge of linguistic principles and theory (e.g., syntactic, semantic, and pragmatic descriptions of language communication); and (4) we are skilled in the application of many clinical techniques related to language use and verbal communication.

Communication therapists still lack comprehensive evaluation strategies, standard methods for specifying verbal interactions between people and for describing their conversational fluency, and a wide variety of remedial methods and materials for overcoming persistent conversational problems. Our clinical experience is steadily accumulating in this area, however, and numerous conversation-based remedial procedures are rapidly being developed. In consideration of our strengths, therefore, we have the potential to help our hearing-impaired clients successfully manage their daily conversations, provided that we carefully and thoughtfully plan our approach to communication therapy.

SUMMARY

Hearing loss can be described at various levels in a hierarchy of disability: sensory, perceptual, interactive, and psycho-social. Similarly, treatment and therapy are available at each of these levels. It is proposed that we apply our accumulating psycho-linguistic knowledge to provide communication therapy at the interactive, or *conversational*, level. This is the level at which most hearing-impaired clients recognize their disability and the level at which they seem to possess the greatest potential for rehabilitation.

2

COMMUNICATION MODEL

In this chapter, we will introduce some of the communication therapy philosophies and procedures which we have developed in our hearing rehabilitation clinics*. Although most of our clients have been *adults with acquired hearing losses*, we feel that a similar conversation-based approach to therapy could be applied successfully with many other people who exhibit receptive or expressive communication disorders. For example, pragmatic approaches to the treatment of *aphasia* have been described (Davis and Wilcox, 1985), and numerous methods for adapting interactive concepts to teaching congenitally *hearing-impaired children* (i.e., those with hearing loss prior to language development) have been proposed (Kretschmer and Kretschmer, 1978; Clezy, 1979).

---

* Our adult hearing rehabilitation clinics are operated by speech-language pathology students under the supervision of a rehabilitative audiologist. These students receive extensive instruction in the theory and practice of speech-language pathology, evaluating and treating clients of all ages who exhibit a wide range of communicative disorders. Their general goals for each client are increased fluency, efficiency, and naturalness in conversation.

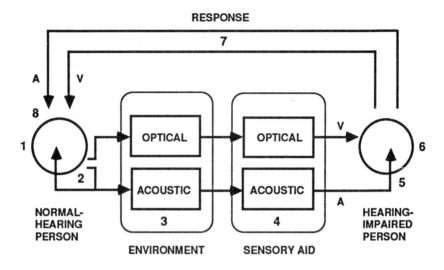

Figure 2-1. Typical model of the communication process (after Erber, 1982).

TALKING HEADS

Before presenting a set of basic procedures for communication therapy, we will examine some general ways in which people appear to interact, both in their own personal lives and in the clinic setting. First, we will consider the simple "talking heads" type of diagram, which theorists commonly use to depict the interaction between communicators.

In most such models of the communication process, a normal-hearing speaker is shown at the left side of the diagram directing a verbal message to another person at the right*, who represents a child or an

---

* In most Western cultures, we habitually tend to treat all printed or graphically depicted events as if they began at the *left* and progressed to the *right*.

adult with a hearing impairment (e.g., see Denes and Pinson, 1973; Bess, Freeman, and Sinclair, 1981). The speaker's mouth may be shown emitting both optical (e.g., mouth movements) and acoustic speech stimuli (e.g., speech sounds), which pass through the surrounding environment(s) to the hearing-impaired person's eyes and ears - via eyeglasses and/or hearing aids, as required (e.g., see Erber, 1982; Figure 2-1). In response, the hearing-impaired person informs the normal-hearing speaker how accurately the spoken messages are being received, thereby prompting further communication.

Many related "talking head" models of human interaction have been proposed, and Sanders (1982) has discussed their evolution. Some of these concepts of the "speech chain" have been relatively simple in structure (Denes and Pinson, 1973) (Figure 2-2a). Others have depicted elaborate parallel systems which represent the complexity of each communicator's contribution (Sanders, 1982) (see Figure 2-2b).

CLINICAL MODEL OF COMMUNICATION

In this text, we present an approach to communication therapy that relies on a somewhat different view of the interactive process. The illustration depicted in Figure 2-3 summarizes some essential features of the specific model of conversation that we apply. As you can see, we have created yet another "talking heads" description of human communication. Superficially, this simple arrangement of heads, boxes, and arrows resembles many of the diagrams which previously have described the now familiar interactive cycle. That is, we also show heads that take turns slinging communication arrows at one another. But several essential differences appear in this model, which was developed specifically for our clinical purposes: there are *four* heads in this diagram, and the head on the *left* (the place where communication "begins") represents the *hearing-impaired* person!

What are the implications of these modifications to the older, more familiar models of communication? Well, we recognize that a conversational interchange between two (or more) people can begin with either (any) one of them. In fact, in real life, we often find it difficult to specify

a.

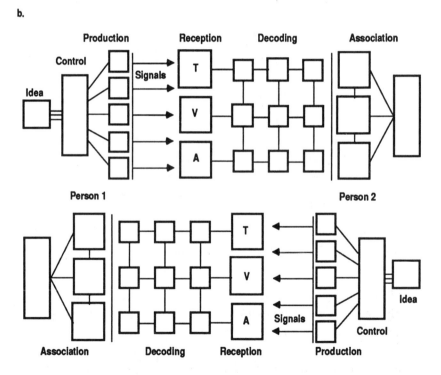

Figure 2-2. Simple (a) and complex (b) models of communication (after Sanders, 1982).

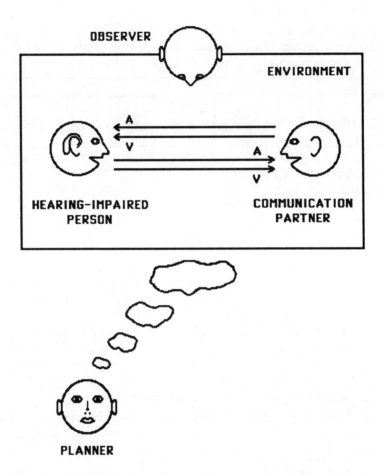

Figure 2-3. New clinical model of the communication process.

the initiator of a particular turn-taking interchange, and thus cannot easily designate the "beginning" of a conversation. For example, the communicator who speaks *first* (e.g., a mother) may actually be *responding* to the other's (e.g., an infant's) nonverbal ("projected"?) intent. A participant (e.g., an apparently dead dog) may even *passively* stimulate the onset of a conversation through his/her/its presence alone (Watzlawick, Bavelas, and Jackson, 1967; see Table 2-1).

Table 2-1. Verbatim transcription of a conversation between a (dead) dog and a (live) human. This example illustrates how difficult it can be to specify the moment at which a conversation begins (i.e., *who* starts it).

Dog:	Human:
(Lies motionless on its side in the middle of a busy university campus walkway. Numerous flies are buzzing around.)	(Exhibits worried facial expression.) "Hello!"..... Are you *dead*?"
(Opens upward-facing eye.)	(Smiles.) Oh! ...... That's good!"
(Wags tail briefly.)	(Exhibits relieved facial expression.) "I hope no one steps on you!"
(Closes eye.)	(Walks away.) "Good-bye!"

In classes for (e.g., hearing-impaired) children, it appears that the (normal-hearing) teacher is the person who begins and maintains most conversations*. Regardless, we and many other clinicians have observed that hearing-impaired people tend to communicate most successfully when *they* can begin and subsequently direct the conversation. This observation does not necessarily mean that the hearing-impaired communicators do all the talking and monopolize all conversations. Rather, it means that they are able to: (1) select or shift topics at will; (2) ask relevant, directive, and response-limiting questions; and/or (3) request specific clarification when necessary. These three actions give them the power to consistently help themselves by narrowing the range of possible con-

---

* One might reasonably claim, however, that the teacher is simply responding to the children's unspoken or implied "questions".

tents, alternatives, and directions of conversations - thus simplifying their perception of speech and their interpretation of spoken messages.

In devising our model for communication, therefore, we have found it both theoretically stimulating and clinically effective to place the hearing-impaired person in the more prominent position on the *left* - as the communicator who suggests topics, makes initiating statements, asks for information, and requests clarification when necessary, that is, the person who is the principal stimulus for verbal communication. Although, as stated, we generally consider the hearing-impaired individual to be the one who *stimulates* responses or requests clarification, the hearing-impaired person may of course *respond* to his/her communication partner's utterances at other times during a conversation.

In this clinical model, the normal-hearing communication partner is shown in the *respondent's* position. That is, we think of the communication partner primarily as a responsive *listener*, receiving the utterances of the hearing-impaired person, and then speaking in response to them. At other times, of course, the normal-hearing person may present or request new information as well.

In these verbal interactions, the two communicators *take turns* as they exchange information. The messages presented by each communicator are judged to contribute equally to the overall communication process (see Sanders, 1982). The result is a basic descriptive model of an ongoing conversation*, where neither the beginning nor the end point is specified.

Two other people also are shown in this general model of communication and communication therapy (Figure 2-3). One is an observer, who appears to the side of the two main interactants (see Cherry, 1966). This individual is able to attend easily to all aspects of the conversation, judge its overall effectiveness and fluency, and guide both communicators. The other person shown is the planner, clinical supervisor, researcher, or

---

* A *conversation* may be described as a purposeful rule-governed exchange of ideas, opinions, or feelings between two or more people (or dogs) (see Davis and Wilcox, 1985).

theorist who has organized and arranged the specific therapeutic interaction that is being observed as it progresses.

You, the clinician, may place yourself in any of these four positions at any given time - in fact, you may have played each of these roles already. Certainly, you have enacted the role of the *communication partner*. This situation is common in most clinical settings, where you as therapist interact verbally with your hearing-impaired clients. You also may have experienced the role of *observer*, for example, projecting, examining, and perhaps guiding communication between a hearing-impaired man and his wife. You may have previously watched and evaluated a video tape recording of one of your own clinical sessions. Or, you may have repeatedly supervised and directed student clinicians in their communication therapy sessions with hearing-impaired adults.

It is likely that you may even have had the opportunity to experience the role of the *hearing-impaired person*, if you have personally experienced a serious conductive hearing loss, have attempted to interact with someone in a very noisy environment, or perhaps have participated in conversation with someone whose expressive communication ability is poor. If you have been fortunate, you may have specifically practised verbal communication while lipreading and simultaneously listening through an electronic hearing loss simulator (Erber, 1985; Gagne and Erber, 1987; also see Chapter 5).

At other times, perhaps before each communication therapy session, you may have assumed the role of *planner*. In this instance, you may have visualized the entire clinical setting and determined how to assist the hearing-impaired client and his/her communication partner most effectively - by guiding each person (perhaps including an *observer*) in his/her designated role.

As you might presume, even a simple conversational interchange appears very different from each point of view. Consequently, one (with normal hearing) can gain a wide variety of insights into the communication problems of hearing-impaired people (and also how to resolve these difficulties), by personally experiencing each role in the communication process - that is, by *being* the hearing-impaired person (simulated), the communication partner, the observer, and the planner of clinical communication therapy sessions.

In the following sections, we will examine the components of the communication process in greater detail. In later chapters, we will show how this model has prompted a new approach to communication therapy for hearing-impaired adults. In the last chapter, we will discuss numerous aspects of communication and communication therapy about which we continue to possess limited knowledge and/or clinical experience, and we will suggest some likely directions for future observation and research.

PERCEPTION AND INTERACTION

The diagram that we have presented in Figure 2-3 illustrates a common conversational or clinical setting, where a hearing-impaired person verbally interacts with another (normal-hearing) communicator. They conduct their conversation within a local environment, defined here by the rectangular border. The hearing-impaired person may have initially triggered the onset of the process by making a statement or by asking a question. When the communication partner responds, that message is conveyed to, and is received by, the hearing-impaired person via optical and acoustic media. That is, the linguistic features of the response are delivered in the form of a changing *acoustic* pattern (which results from laryngeal and vocal tract movement) and also in the form of a changing *optical* pattern of mouth shapes and facial expressions (composed of the unintended visible by-products of acoustic message production) (see Alich, 1967; DeFilippo, 1982a). These parallel streams of vocal information enter the hearing-impaired person's sensory/perceptual systems via eyeglasses, eyes, hearing aids, and impaired ears.

How the hearing-impaired person continues the conversation will depend not only on the clarity of the communication partner's utterance, but also on his/her own personal communicative competence. If unsure of the message content, the hearing-impaired individual might judge the source of the difficulty and then request speech or language clarification, guiding the other communicator to apply appropriate strategies. If correct perception seems likely to have occurred and this is verified, the hearing-impaired person might effectively extend the conversation, by making an elaborative statement or by asking a related question.

In this situation, where one of the communicators is a hearing-impaired person, the turn-taking that occurs within conversations may not always progress smoothly. There may be times when the hearing-impaired person misunderstands - as a result of the other person's speaking habits, distractions in the environment, auditory distortions, or his/her own incorrect assumptions regarding the course of the conversation. These misunderstandings may result in a momentary disruption in the conversation, a brief loss of conversational fluency, a change in topic, or extended and persistent communication breakdown. If these disruptive events frequently cause confusion for the hearing-impaired person and also for that person's regular communication partners, either/both may seek the help of a communication therapist.

PERCEPTUAL DEVELOPMENT

Historically, aural rehabilitation has been directed to the hearing-impaired person's *sensory limitations*, and to the complex *perceptual difficulties* that can result. That is, specialists have applied most of their therapeutic efforts to teaching the hearing-impaired person how to: adapt to his/her hearing aids; manipulate their controls and switches; listen more effectively to amplified speech signals; and also make maximum use of visible cues for lipreading (Hodgson, 1986). Over the years, audiologists have properly selected and adjusted countless hearing aids and earmoulds in assisting hearing-impaired people. In general, these amplification devices have made incoming speech sounds louder, more detectable, and thus potentially recognizable. That is, they have converted many of the previously inaudible or indistinct sounds of speech into acoustic stimuli capable of contributing more efficiently to daily (auditory-visual) communication.

Fluent, interactive speech communication normally requires that one accurately detect, discriminate, identify, and comprehend the speaker's utterances. Auditory training and lipreading instruction both tend to retain *perceptual* orientations for this reason. Through guided experiences, the clinician attempts to enhance the hearing-impaired person's perceptual performance in each modality. Although the various auditory and visual tasks can easily be *combined* in clinical practice (Erber, 1975; Garstecki, 1981a; Danz and Binnie, 1983; Montgomery, Walden, Schwartz, and Prosek, 1984), they are more typically presented in relative isolation from one another (Jeffers and Barley, 1971; Erber, 1982; Sims, 1985).

The sessions may incorporate organized presentations of selected basic speech units (e.g., sounds, mouth shapes). These pre-planned "lessons" usually are ordered along a continuum of perceptual difficulty such as audibility, visibility, low-high frequency content, number of syllables, duration or complexity, and so forth, and they may be selected to promote early success (Urbantschitsch, 1895; Goldstein, 1939; Carhart, 1961). Later tasks typically increase in difficulty, as the clinician introduces longer, more complex, or more obscure speech units which cannot be distinguished so easily (see Kopra, Kopra, Abrahamson, and Dunlop, 1986). The client steadily advances to the limit of his/her auditory and visual perceptual capacity, reaching a level where progress may slow and failure becomes frequent*.

LIMITATIONS OF TRADITIONAL AURAL REHABILITATION

At this point in the clinical process, hearing-impaired clients often lose interest in a traditional aural rehabilitation programme, and many clinicians become frustrated when they find that their effectiveness as therapists is limited. We suggest that there are several reasons that this happens:

(i). Those who created and have sustained the field of aural rehabilitation have tended to be professionals whose basic orientation to hearing, hearing impairment, and treatment of hearing-impairment exists mainly at the sensory/perceptual level (Figure 1-1)*.

---

* For comparison, see the description of an *adaptive* approach to auditory habilitation in Erber (1982)

(ii). Many clinical practitioners continue to provide aural rehabilitation according to the simple stimulus - response - reinforcement paradigm that forms the structure for much classroom teaching. Some clinicians initiate and dominate all interchanges, rather than promoting a balanced interactive process that can be applied in the real world.

(iii). Neither the conversational role of the "other communicator" nor the complex interaction that occurs between communication partners is routinely incorporated into aural rehabilitation theory and practice.

(iv). Even the most basic psycho(socio-)linguistic concepts (e.g., turn-taking rituals; contingent-pair sequences; error identification, problem-solving, and clarification strategies) are rarely considered and applied during traditional aural rehabilitation sessions. As a result, few conversational aspects of human communication are realized and practised as components of most aural rehabilitation programmes.

LINGUISTIC AWARENESS

Of course, as we develop workable plans for therapy, we continue to recognize that hearing impairment is essentially a communication disorder of *sensory/perceptual* origin. And so, we acknowledge the potential value of hearing aids, lipreading instruction, and auditory training to numerous hearing-impaired people. We also, however, recognize that many communication situations exist where one's perceptual limitations cannot be overcome through the use of these traditional aural rehabilitation techniques.

Other methods - ones that are less reliant on impaired *perception* - are needed to minimize the conversational difficulties that inevitably result from sensorineural hearing loss. For example, in the clinical approach to

---

* Even the commonly-used term, *Aural Rehabilitation*, suggests a *perceptual* approach to therapy.

communication therapy that is described in this text, not only do hearing-impaired people learn how to exploit their perceptual capabilities, but they also discover how to examine, direct, and modify their conversations. They gain confidence in guiding the verbal behaviour of their communication partners - so that more spoken language matches their recognized perceptual range. In addition, they learn how to use their latent linguistic knowledge - especially the pragmatic aspects of human communication - to fill any "perceptual gaps" that remain.

In our clinical program, we stress recognition of one's own perceptual capacities and limitations, of one's linguistic skills, and of one's ability to apply language awareness to communication. We concentrate primarily on increasing the client's confidence in application of his/her present linguistic abilities*. That is, we informally evaluate each client's linguistic skills. Then we show how a person's accumulated knowledge of semantics (word associations) and syntax (word-order rules) can be applied to reconstruct utterences when only fragments of messages have been accurately received, and when little sensory information is available for a more complete analysis (see pp. 105-109).

Further, we demonstrate to our hearing-impaired clients how they can use their long-term experience with the interactive patterns of *conversation* to help themselves communicate more easily when their sensory and perceptual mechanisms are inadequate. They discover that they often can anticipate what people will say, or at least they can predict the general form and content of another person's utterance. One often can make such predictions on the basis of: situational contexts that limit message content (e.g., discussion with a bank teller) (see pp. 114-116); knowledge of a communication partner's typical conversational style (e.g., use of jargon, local colloquialisms, gestures); common conversational sequences (e.g., as in greeting rituals); and expected responses to utterances of particular types (e.g., to choice questions) (see pp. 129-138). When the number of possible alternatives is decreased, one's opportuni-

---

* Clinical experience suggests that it is very difficult to substantially increase an adult's overall level of linguistic sophistication.

ties for interpreting verbal communication increases (Sumby and Pollack, 1954).

INTERACTIVE/PRAGMATIC FACTORS

In many traditional models of teaching or therapy, the normal-hearing communication partner is simply referred to as the "speaker" or "talker", and the hearing-impaired communicator is designated as the "listener", "lipreader", or "observer" (see Erber, 1982; Sanders, 1982). The implication is that communication is essentially a directional process, initiated by the normal-hearing person, whose task is to deliver messages to, and obtain responses from, the hearing-impaired communicator. Of course, in real life, the two people are likely to interact socially and participate in a reciprocal *conversation* instead. Real communicators take turns, give and/or get information, and exchange ideas and feelings. We now incorporate these notions into our approach to communication and communication therapy.

Specfic aspects of *conversation* are now being actively studied. For example, numerous researchers have investigated the special speech and pre-speech interactions that take place between parents and their infants (Lewis, 1978; Nienhuys, Cross, and Horsborough,1984; Lyon, 1985), examining message contents as well as many aspects of the turn-taking process. Educators have begun to suggest ways in which awareness of these special interactive patterns can be applied to enhancing fluent communication between parents and their hearing-impaired children (Ling, 1984).

The field of *pragmatics* (the study of language use in a meaningful context) is expanding rapidly. Researchers now routinely document the acquisition of interactive communication abilities in children, including those with hearing impairments and language disorders (Kretschmer and Kretschmer, 1978, 1980; Wiig and Semel, 1984; Griffith, Johnson, and Dastoli, 1985). Others are beginning to examine the complex patterns of verbal interchange that occur during conversations between *adults* (Watzlawick, Bavelas, and Jackson, 1967; DiMatteo and DiNicola, 1982; Pendleton and Hasler, 1983; Stubbs, 1983; McLaughlin, 1984).

As the result of natural development, or perhaps following therapeutic intervention, a person gradually becomes *aware* that he/she communicates by means of linguistic symbols. Many people also learn that they can even consciously observe, describe, and discuss their own communicative acts from a separate, observer's point of view. Psycho-(socio-) linguists have become interested in the ways that people acquire and apply these observational, analytical, or "meta-communicative" abilities. For example, it is now clear that as children mature, they acquire an ability to analyse and assume conscious control over their communicative acts (see Hakes, 1980; Saywitz and Wilkinson, 1982; Pratt and Nesdale, 1984). Some aspects of modern psychotherapy, in fact, rely on a meta-communicative analysis of one's use of and/or *control by* language (Watzlawick, Bavelas, and Jackson, 1967; Perls, 1969; Ellis and Harper, 1975; Okun and Rappaport, 1980).

Unfortunately, there is not a large body of literature that realistically details typical adult-to-adult language interaction (i.e., *conversation*), or that examines the way that adults typically employ their meta-communication (conscious *conversation-analysis*) skills (but see Duncan, 1972, 1973; Sacks, Schegloff, and Jefferson, 1974; Clark and Clark, 1977; Goodwin, 1981). More important for this discussion, we are not aware of any extensive studies of the implications of acquired hearing impairment for *conversation* - that is, the specific ways that hearing impairment affects the naturalness and fluency of interactive adult-to-adult communication (see Stephens, 1980; McCall, 1984).

CLINICAL APPLICATIONS

One major goal of our communication therapy programme has been development of the client's meta-communication skills. For example, we encourage our clients to tell us about their conversational successes (and failures) whenever possible - to increase their awareness of what makes conversations succeed, and to help them discover how they can contribute constructively to the ultimate success of their interactions with others, in spite of the perceptual limitations imposed by their hearing losses. At particular times, in fact, we have intentionally diverted a conversation to specifically discuss the many factors which are causing it to succeed or fail. In like manner, we have reviewed videotapes of clinical conversations to examine the details of the communication acts themselves. We may ask, for example: who's talking most of the time; are both communicators maintaining the topic; are clarification procedures used effectively; are pragmatic conventions being violated?

We routinely incorporate numerous interactive procedures into our communication therapy sessions. These include practice in socially accepted turn-taking procedures: e.g., how to recognize when the other person wants a turn to talk, and when the other communicator is relinquishing his/her turn (see Duncan, 1972, 1973; Gerot, 1977). This can be difficult if one is hearing impaired, as some turn-taking cues are conveyed acoustically, i.e., by pause or intonation (fortunately, most are visible - at least during face-to-face conversation).

We also describe the nature of the many *contingencies* in conversation. We show that certain statements and/or questions spoken by one communication partner tend to specify the general form (and sometimes even the content) of the other's response. For example, a request usually elicits a grant/refusal, and so forth (Clark and Clark, 1977). Later, we provide practice in this special form of turn-taking, showing the hearing-impaired client how the spoken response in each case is often very predictable. As part of this work, we have developed several special question-answer activities (QUEST?AR: Erber, 1985 and pp. 124-129; ASQUE>>>, pp. 129-138), by which the hearing-impaired person gains valuable experience in guiding parts of conversations. A conversation often proceeds most smoothly when the hearing-impaired person asks specific, response-limiting questions.

We also show our clients how they can analyse a conversation while they are *still participating in it*. We have adopted a "problem-solving" approach, in which the hearing-impaired client discovers: how to recognize that a conversation has been disrupted; how to analyse and specify the source of the problem; how to select and apply a clarification strategy; and how to judge the effectiveness of the chosen strategy. Practice may include working out solutions to real conversational difficulties with various communication partners.

THE COMMUNICATION PARTNER

Every conversation involves at least two people. Therefore, to maximize conversational fluency, we also must examine the contribution of the hearing-impaired client's frequent communication partners (e.g., spouse, relatives, friends, and employers) - both as receivers and producers of spoken messages (McCall, 1984).

It is quite common to assist communication partners in cases where they are relatives or friends of a *profoundly* hearing-impaired person, and they desire to learn how to communicate *non-verbally* - through sign language or fingerspelling. It is less common, however, for a similar course of instruction to be created and applied to teaching effective *speech* communication, as many people presume that because they produce non-deviant speech patterns, they are capable of communicating fluently with someone who has acquired a hearing impairment - especially if they are permitted to shout or over-articulate.

We, and most of our adult clients, have observed that, unfortunately, many speakers are not easy to understand. In fact, some speakers are *very poor* verbal communicators. As a result, a hearing-impaired person may neither be able to lipread them easily nor be able to receive their utterances through hearing aids and impaired hearing*. Clinical experience suggests that a speakers' communication failures can be the result of careless articulation, rapid speech rate, fluctuating voice level, accent or dialect, unusual oral/facial structure, use of complex sentence forms, and so forth. These characteristics do not ordinarily cause problems for

---

* Virtually every "normal" speaker is quite intelligible to most others with normal hearing and of course seems especially intelligible to him/herself. The average person is a very poor judge of his/her own speech clarity, however, because the intended message is always *known* as the speech is judged - unless a video tape is made and the speaker examines it at a much later time.

normal-hearing communicators, but they can seriously disrupt conversations for people with hearing impairments, even in quiet, non-distracting environments.

If the hearing-impaired person's frequent communication partners are interested in becoming "clients" themselves, then they also can learn how to contribute to conversational fluency. Numerous methods have been developed for improving one's speech clarity and thus one's intelligibility for hearing-impaired receivers. For example, one may simply listen carefully to his/her own acoustic output during speech production. Unless the speaker is a very experienced, analytical listener, however, it is very unlikely that he/she will be able to accurately judge the quality of the speech that is produced.

Accurate self-assessment of one's speech *visiblity* also can be difficult. Of course, a speaker can examine his/her own visible articulations in a mirror, but this method is poor for judging *intelligibility*, as one's intent while speaking is known. Still, an attentive speaker may use self-observation to gain awareness of which articulators are most prominent and visible, and thus he/she can learn how co-articulation, reduced syllable stress, and high speech rate can obscure the visibility of particular articulatory units. Although it is difficult to make valid judgements regarding the *visibility* of one's own facial features by attending only to internal muscular movement, pressure, or tension while speaking, those kinesthetic cues and feedback *can* contribute once the speaker has become aware of how to achieve speech clarity through other means.

Various electronic instruments can provide valuable information regarding particular speech parameters. For example, we can use a visible speech-feedback device to display one's typical voice pitch, pitch range, or syllable rate on a screen or paper tape. We can use a sound spectrograph to illustrate a speaker's formant patterns, as well as numerous other details: prominence of vowel transitions; strength of the nasal murmur; duration of prevoicing in stops; amount of breathiness; and so forth (Hochberg, Levitt, and Osberger, 1983). Even a sound-level meter held at various distances from the mouth to estimate the acoustic input to someone's hearing aids can assist the speaker in assessing the relative strengths of speech sounds and thus the likelihood of their audibility.

Still, it generally is agreed that if one desires to examine his/her own speech clarity (and thus its potential for intelligibility), then another person must listen, look, and judge its quality. Sometimes a *hearing-impaired* person can contribute relevant suggestions regarding one's audibility and visibility. In our experience, however, the most motivated judge may simply be *another normal-hearing* person with a similar background and purpose as the one desiring feedback - such as another parent, spouse, teacher of hearing-impaired children, or a communication therapist. Ideally, this judge would be someone familiar with the features of clear, intelligible voice and articulation. We have found that this communication partner can provide information and feedback most efficiently if he/she lipreads while listening through a special electronic system that allows simulation of hearing losses of various types (see Chapter 5).

A speaker's intelligibility is not only a function of the precision of visible articulations or the intensity and frequency patterns of the vocal output. The content of what one says also is a vital element. Specific words vary greatly in their auditory and visual intelligibilities to hearing-impaired people (Erber, 1985). Spoken sentences also exhibit a wide range of syntactic complexities. Speakers construct sentences that differ considerably in their internal redundancies (word/phrase associations), and thus their predictabilities. More complicated and longer sentences are known to be harder for a hearing-impaired person to remember, analyse, and/or understand (Schwartz and Black, 1967; Clouser, 1976; Kopra, Kopra, Abrahamson, and Dunlop, 1986). Of course, a speaker who wishes to maximize intelligibility to a hearing-impaired person can study prepared lists of visible and/or audible sentences. Our clinical experience suggests, however, that it is easier to acquire this knowledge through realistic practice and interactive *experience* than through *study* alone - an observation which is consistent with what is known about styles of adult learning (O'Neil, 1978; Lovell, 1980).

To maximize understanding, a normal-hearing speaker also can apply many of the same principles that are commonly followed by hearing-impaired communicators. For example, one is likely to be most easily understood if he/she talks about topics that are familiar to, and even suggested by, the hearing-impaired person, although if followed exclusively, this approach may be constricting and unsatisfying for both communicators. Of course, one also can increase intelligibility by employing language (including local colloquial expressions and/or well-known jargon) that is familiar to, and also is commonly used by, the hearing-impaired person.

If the normal-hearing communication partner persists in presenting long narratives (monologues), the hearing-impaired person is likely to experience considerable difficulty. A hearing-impaired adult can cope with this type of conversation, however, if he/she is permitted to periodically guide the interchange (e.g., by asking directive questions and/or requesting clarification), and if the normal-hearing communicator recognizes and cooperates with this approach. If the topic has been suggested by a situation within the surrounding environment, then frequent references to people, objects, or events nearby (e.g., pointing or gesturing to designate the referent) often can assist in clarification.

Other important considerations are topic identification and topic maintenance (Jeffers and Barley, 1971). It is much easier for a hearing-impaired person to participate interactively if the speaker unambiguously identifies the topic when beginning the conversation ("On Sunday, we visited my friend who lives in Healesville."), and also clearly signals whenever introducing another topic (e.g., "Now, please tell me about your new grandson").

SUMMARY

In this chapter, we have oriented the reader to some of the communication therapy philosophies and procedures that are described throughout the text, and have briefly explained the rationale for their application. Rehabilitation for adults with acquired hearing losses is no longer simply a matter of fitting hearing aids, counselling, providing listening practice, and teaching lipreading. The *conversational process* itself has become the vehicle for therapy. We anticipate that ongoing research on pragmatics and meta-communication will help us organize newly developed therapeutic procedures into a cohesive clinical programme.

3

CLINICAL PROCEDURES

CONVERSATION-BASED THERAPY

In this chapter, we will present an overview of our communication therapy programme for hearing-impaired adults. This rehabilitative approach is based partly on procedures originally created for *telephone* instruction, in which *conversations* provide the framework for clinical interaction (Erber, 1985). The process also is derived partly from clinical formats previously suggested by Hull, (1976), Binnie (1976), Garstecki (1981a, b), Sanders (1982), Bode, Tweedie, and Hull (1982), Erber (1982), and Davis and Wilcox (1985).

Five main clinical activities are included:

(1) conduct **professional conversations** with the client: that is, acquire a general impression of his/her purposes and needs (interview, obtain a case history, administer a questionnaire, observe communication efficiency); orient the client to the clinical programme; administer brief perceptual screening tests; discuss the test results; and plan/revise an individualized therapy programme;

(2) conduct limited, **simulated conversations** with the client, playing typical communicator roles in realistic environments; analyse and discuss significant communication events that occur during this interaction;
(3) obtain a detailed **assessment** of the client's perceptual and language-use abilities by administering specific diagnostic tests;
(4) direct **communication practice** to selected (deficient) component skills; provide information, counselling, and guidance;
(5) if possible, observe, analyse, and discuss the client's participation in **personal conversations** with frequent communication partners under typical environmental conditions.

At each stage in the process, the communication therapist must carefully consider the client's expressed objectives as well as his/her demonstrated needs.

BOXES AND ARROWS

Typical Clinical Sequence

We usually follow a prescribed sequence throughout a series of clinical sessions. This process is presented in the form of a "flow chart" (Figure 3-1).

Many flow charts that serve as clinical models tend to resemble one another. They generally depict the client's entrance to the programme at the top of the diagram and his/her exit at the bottom. In between, the various clinical processes are applied in order, one beneath the other (for example, see Ling, 1976; Goldstein and Stephens, 1981; Erber, 1982; Montgomery, Walden, Schwartz, and Prosek, 1984; Sims, 1985). According to these models, a typical hearing-impaired client experiences this sequence of events: intake, interview, diagnostic testing, therapy, evaluation of therapy, discharge.

There is nothing inherently wrong with this idealized approach to the organization of "treatment" for a hearing-impaired client, but it does have certain drawbacks. For example, many current diagnostic procedures may neither be sufficiently sensitive to, nor even be related to, the client's reported difficulties in conversation. Provision of therapy usually is deferred until testing is complete; at that point, some test results may be found to be irrelevant. Also, some clients may abandon an aural rehabilitation programme after only a few visits - because they experience nothing but *assessment* during initial sessions. If the client does leave the programme before completion, he/she may acquire little feeling of accomplishment, and the clinician may receive little feedback regarding the outcome of whatever minimal therapy has been provided. Moreover, this sort of idealized linear clinical model is a poor description of what many skilled communication therapists actually do. It is more an analogue of classroom teaching (or a gravity-powered industrial process) than a description of clinical practice.

We have developed a model for communication therapy that overcomes many of these objections - one which we feel is conceptually more desirable and descriptively more accurate. In Figure 3-1, we have depicted the sequence applied in our clinic, where increased *conversational fluency* is a primary objective. Superficially, the plan described by this flow chart resembles the teaching model referred to above, but it differs in several important ways. For example, one's exit from communication therapy takes place at the point of origin - shown here at the top of the diagram. Moreover, specific testing to confirm and/or diagnose the client's expressed and/or demonstrated communication difficulties is carried out relatively late in the overall clinical process.

The clinical process is divided into two main segments, separated here by a horizontal dashed line (Figure 3-1). This boundary separates communication therapy into events that take place in the client's familiar, real world (e.g., home, office, factory, car, restaurant) and events that occur in the clinic - which is a somewhat artificial, hopefully therapeutic world. The client begins the entire sequence by communicating in the real world, and later returns to it. In fact, the client returns periodically - each time he/she completes a communication therapy session and emerges from the clinic.

Let us consider each of the steps outlined in Figure 3-1. The process begins when a hearing-impaired individual engages in real, personal conversations within his/her own home or work environment. If no

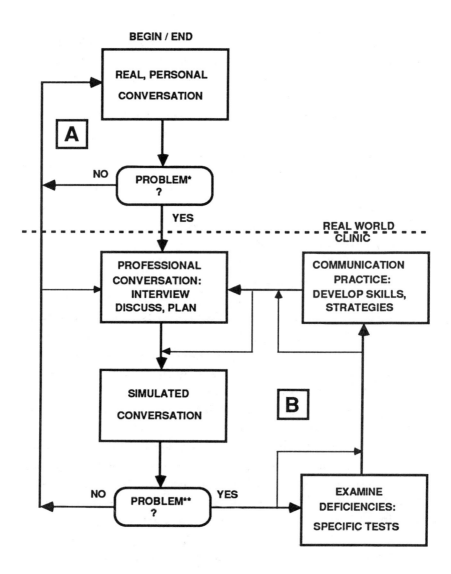

* judged by client and/or communication partner

** judged by client and/or clinician

Figure 3-1. The communication therapy process.

difficulties are experienced, little change in lifestyle occurs. That is, the person simply continues to participate in routine conversations with family, friends, and co-workers. Every day, he/she repeatedly traverses this loop, with no apparent, recognized communication problems. The hearing-impaired person's hearing loss, in fact, may not cause sufficient difficulty to worry him/her, although communication partners may be (very) aware of their frequent need for repetition or clarification.

Time passes. The hearing impairment worsens, and received speech becomes less audible and/or less clear. The person (or the family) may become much more aware of recurrent dysfluencies in conversation. Numerous repetitions and frequent clarifications may be required. Achieving (near-) normal continuity may demand a great amount of conscious effort. Regardless of the reason, the hearing-impaired person may gradually (or suddenly) recognize that conversational fluency and naturalness have begun to diminish, and that he/she has a significant communication problem. This realization may lead to a personal decision to obtain communication therapy.

The hearing-impaired person has chosen to cross the boundary into the domain of the communication therapy clinic. Here, our first step usually is a "professional conversation" - to interview and orient the hearing-impaired individual, obtain a case history, and establish the reasons why the person has requested help.

It is quite common to obtain extremely detailed information about the client's pure-tone thresholds, word-identification abilities, and hearing-aid requirements. Beyond these quantitative audiometric data, however, the communication therapist also will want to find out how the person feels about his/her hearing impairment. Thus, during their initial conversation, the clinician and the hearing-impaired client will discuss the client's recognized communication difficulties, his/her goals for therapy, and consider how each person might play a role in the subsequent rehabilitation process. The organization of the clinic, its facilities, its philosophy, and its staff and their areas of expertise all are explained. The clinician briefly summarizes the communication therapy programme, and describes the sequence of events that might occur during a typical weekly session (e.g., simulated conversations, listening/lipreading practice, problem-solving, application of clarification strategies).

It is likely that the initial encounter will include a comprehensive interview (see Table 3-1). At this time, the hearing-impaired person is asked to describe the effects of his/her own hearing loss on personal communication and life style. The individual is encouraged to discuss the conditions under which negative effects on communication are most noticeable, such as in groups, in noisy places, or over the telephone. Specific questions are asked about the character of typical "problem conversations": communication partner, purpose, topic, content, duration, location, and so forth (Hull, 1980; Davis and Wilcox, 1985) (see Table 3-2). The clinician enquires about previous treatments, counselling, and therapy, and attempts to determine how much the client understands about his/her hearing disability. The client's expectations for, and experience with, amplification devices also are surveyed. During this time, the client's auditory and visual speech-perception abilities and speech quality are observed. The clinician notes any obvious difficulties that occur in conversation, and also considers the client's apparent knowledge and use of remedial communication strategies.

A brief self-assessment scale also may be administered, such as the Hearing Handicap Inventory for the Elderly (HHIE) (Ventry and Weinstein, 1982, 1983; Weinstein and Ventry, 1983; Weinstein, Spitzer, and Ventry, 1986) (Table 3-3a,b). The application of such questionnaires has been extensively reviewed by Alpiner and McCarthy (1987). In general, these clinical procedures tell us something about the client's personal attitudes and general psycho-social and vocational adjustment, indicate areas where the client feels that the hearing impairment has become a "handicap", and yield diagnostic data to guide communication therapy. The information they provide also helps to confirm the results of the less structured, but more personal, interview.

Following this, perhaps at the next session, brief auditory and visual screening tests may be administered - to gain some knowledge of the

Table 3-1. Components of communication therapy.

I. Interview client
   A. Characteristics and effects of hearing loss
   B. Related medical/personal factors
   C. Previous use of hearing aid(s) or other devices
   D. Previous aural rehabilitation or communication therapy
   E. Reasons for attending clinic: information, hearing-aid orientation, learn lipreading/listening, conversational fluency, telephone use
   F. Discuss nature of typical "problem conversation": communication partner, conversational format and context:
      1. Who? (e.g., family member, friend, co-worker, shop assistant)
      2. What? (e.g., topic, content, vocabulary, language, structure)
      3. Why? (e.g., give/get information, maintain friendship, gossip)
      4. Where? (e.g., home, factory, meeting; acoustic/optical distractions)
      5. How long? (e.g., brief contact, narrative, long discussion)
   G. Administer self-assessment questionnaire (e.g., HHIE)
   H. Informally note conversational fluency
   I. Describe clinic and typical procedures

II. Screen client's speech-perception abilities and discuss.
   A. Visual (e.g., LIST I)
   B. Auditory (e.g., LIST II and LIST III; high-frequency word list)
   C. Auditory-visual (e.g., SENT-IDENT)

III. Conduct simulated conversation(s) with client (e.g., TOPICON), playing role of typical communication partner. Assess conversational fluency; note instances and causes of communication breakdown; discuss effects of topic and client's use of strategies.

IV. Administer specific tests and discuss results. Assist client (and friends/family) in remediation of deficient communication abilities. Provide communication practice, information, counselling, or referral.
   A. Lipreading and/or auditory skills
   B. Use of hearing aids, telephone, and other devices
   C. Language knowledge and use; meta-communication skills
   D. Problem identification and problem-solving; clarification strategies
   E. Control of environmental distractors
   F. Communication partner's role

V. If possible, observe real conversations between client and frequent communication partners, in which client attempts to apply newly learned skills. Discuss conversational occurrences.

Table 3-2. Assessing particular communication problems and their relative importance to hearing-impaired adults (after Hull, 1980). A hearing-impaired adult's responses are shown.

Do you have difficulty when communicating:

	No	Sometimes	Yes	Priority
With males		✓		
With females		✓		
With children		✓		
With particular people		✓		
In groups			✓	2
At work		✓		
At home		✓		
At dinner			✓	4
While shopping	✓			
At meetings			✓	1
At the theatre	✓			
At social events			✓	5
In a car		✓		
On the telephone			✓	3
Other (specify)				

client's general ability to see, hear, and receive speech (see pp. 61-72). Syllables, words, and/or sentences may be presented as test stimuli. Together, the clinician and the client examine the client's basic perceptual strengths and weaknesses.

Next, the client's ability to communicate interactively is sampled, observed, and evaluated - usually during the second session. A brief simulated conversation is organized and enacted between the client and the clinician - on a topic chosen from a prepared list (e.g., a recent visit from my cousin; the new supermarket in your neighborhood; life on other planets: see TOPICON, pp. 75-85). This conversation may be held within a potentially disruptive environment (e.g., during lunch at a noisy restaurant; in traffic noise at a nearby bus stop; over the telephone; sitting side-by-side in a moving car) that also is simulated, with the clinican playing the role of a typical communication partner. Alternatively, conversational *fragments* may be presented in these simulated (or real-life) situations. For example, either communicator may be required to obtain answers to a series of questions (see QUEST?AR, pp. 124-129; ASQUE>>>, pp.129-138). During this evaluation, the clinician notes any communication conditions which consistently disrupt the conversation (e.g., noise, rapid speech rate, long sentences), or which stimulate the hearing-impaired client to apply effective/ineffective remedial strategies (e.g., noise avoidance; requests for clarification) (see pp. 116-124).

For example, the hearing-impaired person may experience great difficulty perceiving speech in background noise. Under these conditions, he/she may not be able to identify certain key words containing weak high-frequency consonants, such as *chicken, artichoke,* or *lychee*. The client may make numerous non-specific requests for clarification (e.g., "What?"; "Pardon?"), or may incorrectly identify the presumed source(s) of error (e.g., the client asks, "Could you speak *louder* please?", when you actually are speaking too *rapidly*). The client may neglect to ask confirming questions when he/she is unsure (such as, "Did you say that your neighbourhood supermarket has a special *Asian foods* section?").

If the client exhibits few (or no) communication problems during either the interview or the simulated conversation(s), then the clinician may resume discussion with the client, explaining that it has been difficult to demonstrate any of the client's reported difficulties. The client may suggest how to modify the clinic conditions to simulate a difficult situation more accurately - in order to cause the communication problems to become more evident and observable. Another simulated conversation may follow. The clinician may: introduce a talker with a higher-pitched voice; may speak more quickly; may increase noise level or reverberation; may reduce visible cues, as over the telephone; or may conduct the session later in the afternoon, when the client is fatigued.

Table 3-3. Screening form of the Hearing Handicap Inventory for the Elderly (HHIE-S: modified slightly from Ventry and Weinstein, 1983). Self-assessments obtained from two hearing-impaired adults: (a) A.T., who felt that he typically experienced little communication difficulty; and (b) F.P., who reported frequent communication breakdowns.

	a. A.T. Yes/Sometimes/No	b. F.P. Yes/Sometimes/No
Does a hearing problem cause you to feel embarrassed when meeting new people?	__ __ ✓	✓ __ __
Does a hearing problem cause you to feel frustrated when talking to members of your family?	__ ✓ __	__ ✓ __
Do you have difficulty hearing when someone speaks in a whisper?	✓ __ __	✓ __ __
Do you feel handicapped by a hearing problem?	__ __ ✓	__ ✓ __
Does a hearing problem cause you difficulty when visiting friends or relatives?	__ ✓ __	__ ✓ __
Does a hearing problem cause you to attend meetings less often than you would like?	__ ✓ __	✓ __ __
Does a hearing problem cause you to have arguments with family members?	__ __ ✓	__ __ ✓
Does a hearing problem cause you difficulty when listening to radio or when watching TV?	__ ✓ __	__ ✓ __
Do you feel that any difficulty with your hearing limits your personal or social life?	__ __ ✓	__ ✓ __
Does a hearing problem cause you difficulty when in a restaurant with friends or relatives?	__ __ ✓	✓ __ __

Again, no significant difficulties may be apparent, even in potentially difficult environments. Further investigation may reveal the following: (1) the client is overly concerned with correctly receiving *every* speech unit in a conversation, although significant breaks in continuity are not apparent. (2) The client exhibits no conversational difficulties, but is greatly stressed by the (simulated) adverse surroundings, and must exert great effort to communicate in an outwardly normal manner. (3) The client demonstrates no current communication problems, but suspects/anticipates a progressive hearing loss and desires counselling to avert conversational difficulties in the future. In each case, we help the client to describe his/her goals for rehabilitation more precisely, or we may ask the client to return to the "real world" to re-examine and redefine the communication problem.

If the hearing-impaired client has exhibited obvious communication problems, however, and meets other clinic-acceptance criteria, then the client is offered a series of therapy sessions. Presumably, the clinician has noted which specific communication difficulties have persistently occurred during the simulated conversations. Later, the clinician may provide instruction and practice on corresponding component skills - before returning to enact other simulated conversations.

In the next step, the clinician assesses the client's communication skills more carefully - especially those observed to be deficient during simulated conversations (see Davis and Wilcox, 1985). For example, some tests may include: effective hearing aid use; auditory perception of words containing high-frequency consonants; auditory-visual perception of sentences; ability to identify sources of difficulty in spoken messages; or ability to use knowledge of language to fill perceptual gaps.

Instruction and practice on related component skills follow. Our decisions regarding the choice of specific content will depend on the nature of the difficulties that previously were noted during conversation or assessment. Practice usually is provided by means of various *interactive* procedures (see pp.109-142).

Following each practice activity, the hearing-impaired client and the clinician conduct a "professional" conversation. At this point, they discuss what they have attempted and accomplished, and together, they consider subsequent steps in the therapeutic process.

Loop A and Loop B

Two "loops" are shown in Figure 3-1. Loop A represents successful real-world communication. Remaining in, or re-entering, this loop is the hearing-impaired person's goal. A hearing-impaired communicator who circles this loop repeatedly is one who is experiencing success in real conversations (i.e., is having relatively few communication problems during conversations with inexperienced communication partners in moderately noisy or distracting environments). Such a person either may have no need for *communication* therapy, or if already involved, he/she may be ready to leave the rehabilitation programme.

Loop B represents the clinical rehabilitation process, including its simulated conversations. The client and the clinician traverse this loop repeatedly until either the clinician judges that few or insignificant communication problems remain, effective strategies for overcoming difficulties have been developed, the client chooses to leave the therapy programme, or after an agreed-upon number of sessions have occurred. A hearing-impaired person who repeatedly circles Loop B is one who is experiencing persistent communication difficulty with particular conversational formats or environmental conditions. Entering and remaining in this loop (i.e., the communication therapy process) for a greatly extended length of time is considered undesirable.

You can help a hearing-impaired person emerge from Loop B in several ways: (1) by providing practice with the most appropriate and significant component skills (e.g., asking questions with limited-choice answers; or identifying the source of difficulty and requesting clarification - rather than practicing syllable- or word-identification); (2) by relaxing the criteria which define the existence of a continuity "problem" (e.g., allow a greater proportion of time during conversations for *clarification*); or (3) by intentionally communicating at a lower level of conversational difficulty - with regard to talker, topic, format, length, vocabulary, and/or amount of background noise (e.g., requesting information from a close relative about a family picnic that is planned for next weekend - a familiar person and a familiar topic) (see Erber, 1985).

Problems that occur during simulated conversations may require application of a wide range of specific remedial procedures (via Loop B)

(see Figure 3-1). For example, the clinician may:
* obtain more specific diagnostic information (e.g., administer a test of language performance);
* recommend hearing-aid adjustment (e.g., modify frequency response);
* introduce the client to special amplification devices (e.g., an acoustic-to-electromagnetic telephone adapter);
* provide specific listening or lipreading practice (e.g., comprehension of sentences containing embedded clauses);
* provide practice with clarification requests (e.g., identifying sources of conversational difficulty and appropriately guiding the communication partner toward clarification);
*demonstrate specific conversation-management strategies (e.g., verifying topic; asking response-limiting questions).

Some of these remedial clinical procedures are methods of assessment, some require application of special apparatus, some pertain to perceptual development, some suggest increased use of latent linguistic skills, and some require (re-)direction of the other communicator. These various activities are described in greater detail in later sections.

Special Features

This overall approach to rehabilitation is unconventional in several ways:
(1) the contents of each session are organized differently (often improvised) according to each hearing-impaired client's current abilities, interests, and needs;
(2) therapy does not follow a "linear sequential" model, where each hearing-impaired client receives the same experiences in a prescribed order; instead, we employ an "ascending spiral" or "helix", often apparently following the same pathway as before, but each time at a higher level of performance or communicative awareness (see Dance, 1967);
(3) because the client accumulates a range of useful communication skills during each therapy session, the client or the clinician may terminate the rehabilitation programme at any time with the satisfaction that some degree of progress has been achieved; although a complete "course" is desired, it is not considered essential;

(4) traditional perception-based therapies, such as hearing aid use, auditory training, and lipreading instruction are applied along with other remedial procedures, but are not given principal status;

(5) most of the clinical assessment and practice activities are *conversation*-oriented, and therefore reflect real life - an approach which tends to appeal to both clients and clinicians (Davis and Wilcox, 1985);

(6) most communication therapists learn these conversation-oriented activities quickly and easily, because the procedures tap their intuitive concepts of human communication as well as extend their existing theoretical knowledge and clinical skills.

HEARING AIDS

We do not treat hearing-aid selection, purchase, and/or use as essential components of the clinical process, although these are principal features of most aural rehabilitation programmes (Hardick and Gans, 1982; Hodgson, 1986). Instead, we realistically accept the fact that many hearing-impaired adults choose *not* to employ hearing aids regularly for verbal communication (Kapteyn, 1977 a,b,c; Surr, Schuchman, and Montgomery, 1978; Franks and Beckmann, 1985).

There are many reasons for non-use of hearing aids (see Table 3-4). For example, the hearing-impaired person may be overly concerned with the small change in physical appearance created by the hearing aids. Others may be disturbed by the symbolism of these devices, which many people continue to associate with old age (Iler, Danhauer, and Mulac, 1982; Mulac, Danhauer, and Johnson, 1983). Still other hearing-impaired people may feel that the overall benefit to their auditory-visual communication is just not worth the added bother of battery replacement, earmould cleaning, routine maintenance, or annoyance from continuously amplified environmental noises (Surr, Schuchman, and Montgomery, 1978; Franks and Beckmann, 1985). We acknowledge that in some cases, especially with elderly clients, the benefit may actually *not* be worth the bother. The clinician should avoid imposing guilt or other negative feelings if the client chooses not to use hearing aids.

Other hearing-impaired adults claim that their hearing aids make speech and other acoustic stimuli (e.g., music) sound "terrible", especially in the presence of background noise (Franks, 1982). That is, although someone's hearing aids produce little electroacoustic distortion, they may make particular sounds audible, which the hearing-impaired person cannot process and whose acoustic qualities he/she cannot perceive with clarity (Corso, 1977; Hayes and Jerger, 1979; Murray and Byrne, 1986). Consequently, the individual may prefer listening *unaided* to a more limited range of sound frequencies and intensities, which at least sound more pleasant - even if they do not contribute maximally to perception of *speech*.

For these many reasons, we do not insist that every one of our hearing-impaired clients obtain, purchase, or use hearing aids to qualify for communication therapy. We do give each person repeated opportunities to communicate while listening to amplified sound, however, illustrating how he/she might benefit under conditions of hearing aid use. Regardless of an individual's current attitudes toward the use of amplification, we still can provide each person with useful information, a variety of appropriate conversation-management techniques, and a range of problem-solving skills.

Pre-Aid Counselling

Some of our clients already have decided to obtain/purchase a hearing aid (or aids), based upon the recommendation of an audiologist or another hearing health-care professional. We normally do not wait until the client actually has possession of his/her hearing aid(s) before beginning the rehabilitation programme. Instead, we usually begin pre-aid counselling immediately, helping the client develop realistic expectations for hearing aid use.

Many potential hearing aid users have been greatly influenced by commercial advertising, and consequently they often expect modern hearing aids to miraculously reverse or eliminate their hearing losses (Erber, 1986). Numerous people, in fact, have overcome their initial reluctance or embarrassment over the wearing of hearing aids as the result of these exaggerated promises regarding the potential contribution of the devices to speech communication. Such clients need to be advised more realistically of the likely benefits and limitations of hearing

Table 3-4. Reasons that many hearing-impaired people claim they do not obtain or use hearing aids.

Earmoulds can feel uncomfortable.

Earmoulds contribute to an accumulation of cerumen in the ear canals.

External otitis or a skin disorder makes use of earmoulds painful.

They have poor manual dexterity, and thus find hearing-aid controls hard to operate.

They feel that battery insertion and earmould cleaning are too annoying and difficult.

Hearing aids, batteries, and repairs are too expensive.

When amplified, speech and music sound harsh and unpleasant.

When amplified, many environmental noises are annoying, such as one's own footsteps, traffic, clattering dishes, or a toilet flushing.

When amplified, many sudden loud noises are frightening, such as a dog barking.

Continuously amplified background noises are a constant distraction.

They do not need hearing aids for face-to-face conversations in *quiet* places, and hearing aids contribute little in group discussions, where background noise and reverberation are present.

aids (Hodgson, 1986). They also should be given experience in listening through several appropriate hearing aids - under various realistic environmental conditions (Oja and Schow, 1984).

They may discover that they can detect and understand speech much more easily with hearing aids than without them, although they still cannot hear speech with clarity - even in quiet surroundings (at least as they remember speech to have sounded before, when their hearing was more normal). When a significant level of background noise is present,

Table 3-4 continued

They notice little difference in quality between aided and unaided (audio-visual) speech-perception.

They believe that the use of powerful hearing aids may damage their hearing further.

They believe that the use of hearing aids may create dependency on hearing for communication. They feel that this can be a potential problem if their hearing is likely to deteriorate further.

They don't want other people to know that they have a hearing loss.

They believe that only very *deaf* people wear hearing aids, and/or they think that others believe this. They don't want anyone to think that they are *deaf*.

They believe that hearing aids are symbols of a loss of youth and an intact body.

They believe that only *old* people use hearing aids, and they don't want other people to think that they are *old*.

They believe that hearing aids make people appear "different" and thus undesirable.

They believe that hearing aids make people appear less attractive to the opposite sex.

They don't want people to treat them as if they were *handicapped*, i.e., patronise them.

They don't want to admit to themselves (be reminded) that they have a hearing loss.

they may find that the acoustic output of hearing aids can be very annoying and confusing, and that amplification may contribute little to their auditory-visual perception of speech. In summary, each hearing-impaired client should become aware that the new hearing aid(s) which he/she is about to receive will bring both benefits and limitations.

Post-Fitting Considerations

Clients who already have (e.g., just recently) received or purchased hearing aids may need some advice on how to adjust to the particular auditory effects that the aids produce. It is best that this (re-) introduction to sound be a gradual process, with the hearing-impaired client first attempting conversations with only one other person in a quiet, non-distracting place. Later, the client may attempt conversations in small groups, where the presence (and the noise) of other people is potentially distracting or even disruptive (Hodgson, 1986). A common problem may occur when the hearing-impaired person briefly withdraws from a group conversation, and merely observes and listens to others communicating. Under these conditions, one must constantly be aware of who is speaking at each moment, so that auditory and visual attention can be directed to the speaker at all times. This constant re-orientation can be very tiring.

Many hearing-impaired people are not sure how to use their hearing aids effectively during *telephone* conversations. Simply switching the hearing aid to the T (telecoil) input position may not resolve the client's telephone-communication problems, if the telephone receiver generates a very weak electro-magnetic field or if the telecoil circuit in the hearing aid is not functioning properly (see Castle, 1980; Erber, 1985). The clinician also may need to explain to the hearing-impaired person how speech energy can be transferred most successfully from the telephone - via the hearing aid - to one's ear (e.g., acoustically, or electro-magnetically). One may specifically recommend: (1) that the client obtain a special telephone with a built-in amplifier (e.g., supplied by the telephone company); (2) that a supplementary induction coil be installed in the telephone receiver to increase the strength of the electro-magnetic energy produced by the telephone receiver (again, provided by the telephone company); and/or (3) that the client purchase a portable adapter to transform weak sound output from the receivers of unconverted telephones to strong electro-magnetic signals for efficient use by the hearing aid (when set to the T position).

EXAMINING PERCEPTUAL ABILITIES

Often, when admitted to a communication therapy programme, a hearing-impaired adult will already be using both audition and vision efficiently for perception of vocal patterns and articulated sequences of speech sounds. This is a common occurrence in an adult who has experienced a gradually acquired, long-term hearing loss. That is, he/she will tend to listen carefully (through correctly adjusted hearing aids) while intently watching the speaker's mouth and face for visible speech cues. Occasionally, however, one may encounter a hearing-impaired client who does not reliably watch the speaker's mouth during conversation. Instead, when unsure, this person may tilt his/her better ear toward the speaker (breaking visual contact), or he/she may look toward the speaker's *eyes* (perhaps to judge affect or intent) or toward the speaker's *hands* (for gestural information). The clinician can help in either case by demonstrating the advantages of relying on combined auditory and visual cues for speech perception. For example, one may show how the visible place cues for stop consonants (bilabial, alveolar, velar) can help to clarify the acoustic ambiguity of /p,t,k/ as in the words *pan*, *tan*, and *can* or /b,d,g/ as in the words *bet*, *debt*, and *get*.

Conversely, the clinician may encounter adult clients who do not use their hearing aids regularly, or who do not set the gain high enough to adequately receive the typical acoustic levels of conversational speech*. The client may report that he/she doesn't like the way speech sounds when it is greatly amplified, perhaps as the result of auditory distortions**. The clinician may be able to help the hearing-impaired person recognize the potential advantages of using the amplification system

---

* Many people claim that the loudness of environmental noise or the sounds of their own (amplified) speech are uncomfortable, and so they decrease the gain of their hearing aids.

** It also is possible that the hearing aid(s), tubing, and/or earmoulds have been incorrectly selected or adjusted, producing unwanted resonances or other undesirable acoustic effects.

regardless - by showing him/her that many visually similar speech units such as syllables or words (e.g., *pad, bad,* and *mad*) can be clarified easily by listening to the (even distorted) amplified speech patterns that accompany the speaker's visible articulations (Erber, 1972).

LIST I: Screening Visual Identification of Consonants

Even when they listen carefully, many people with serious hearing losses are not able to reliably detect, discriminate, and/or identify weak, high-frequency consonants (Bailey, 1983). As a result, they often attend visually to the speaker's mouth and face for complementary/compensatory cues - mainly to specify consonant mouth shapes and identify visible places of consonant articulation*.

Often, we want to evaluate a hearing-impaired adult's ability to "read lips". In some instances, we simply want to know how well the person can visually distinguish the variety of mouth configurations, that are called "visemes" (see Fisher, 1968)**. These visible articulatory units are believed by many to be the symbols that convey linguistic information from the speaker to the lipreader (see Alich, 1967). Each viseme (distinctive mouth configuration) represents a set of vowels or consonants which may sound very different, but whose visible articulations look essentially the same (e.g., /t, d, n, s, z/), even when spoken carefully to experienced lipreaders.

These similarities in visible appearance occur because certain speech-feature distinctions which characterize each sound as voiced/voiceless or nasal/non-nasal are produced deep within the speaker's vocal tract

---

* It is likely that in most cases of acquired hearing loss, in which auditory *vowel* perception is not seriously impaired, the individual uses visible vowel information mainly to confirm what is perceived acoustically through hearing aids and impaired ears (but see Hack and Erber, 1982; Nabelek and Letowski, 1985).

** This approach to testing visual perception is somewhat analogous to assessing a person's visual acuity by displaying static letters on a chart at a 6 metre distance. In this case, however, the test stimuli are dynamic, three-dimensional articulatory images presented at a conversational distance (e.g., 1 metre).

and thus cannot be seen externally. Investigators disagree on the exact number of visemes (distinctive mouth shapes) in spoken English, probably as the result of studying different talkers, lighting conditions, articulatory contexts, and so forth (Jeffers and Barley, 1971).

Many tests of visual perception of speech have incorporated a large number of consonant stimuli, usually spoken in initial position before the open, "rounded" vowel /a/ (see Pesonen, 1968; Erber, 1972; Plant, 1980). Responses to these stimuli by experienced lipreaders usually yield the typical clusterings referred to earlier (e.g., /p,b,m/, /f,v/, /θ,ð/, and so forth). Given the stability of these typical results, Binnie, Jackson, and Montgomery, (1976) proposed a lipreading screening test composed of 20 consonants paired with the vowel /a/, and randomly presented five times each (100 total items). We have found that this lipreading screening test provides useful diagnostic information, but that it takes a considerable amount of time to administer, and the results are partly predictable (e.g., as one might expect, most people consistently confuse /p/ with /b/).

Only *unusual* lipreading (i.e., visual perception) errors are informative to the clinician. Therefore, to obtain similar results more efficiently, we have condensed the screening format, and now present only *eight* consonants (/dʒ, w, b, v, ð, l, d, g/), each representing a specific viseme*. Each consonant is spoken without voice in an "easy" bisyllabic (/a/-C-/a/) context five times in random order (40 total items). The client's responses are recorded on an 8 x 8 matrix (see Figure 3-2).

Careful articulation by an experienced clinician (under frontal, mouth-level lighting conditions) usually results in perfect identification of the 40 items by lipreaders who are very attentive and somewhat analytical**. Any errors that do result (i.e., denoting confusions *between* the viseme classes) represent perceptual and/or analytical deficiencies -

---

* For example, we acknowledge that /p/ and /m/ would be confused visually with /b/, and so we present only /b/.

** Occasionally, however, confusions do occur between /d/ and /g/, both of which are *postdental* articulations and thus can be very similar in surface appearance.

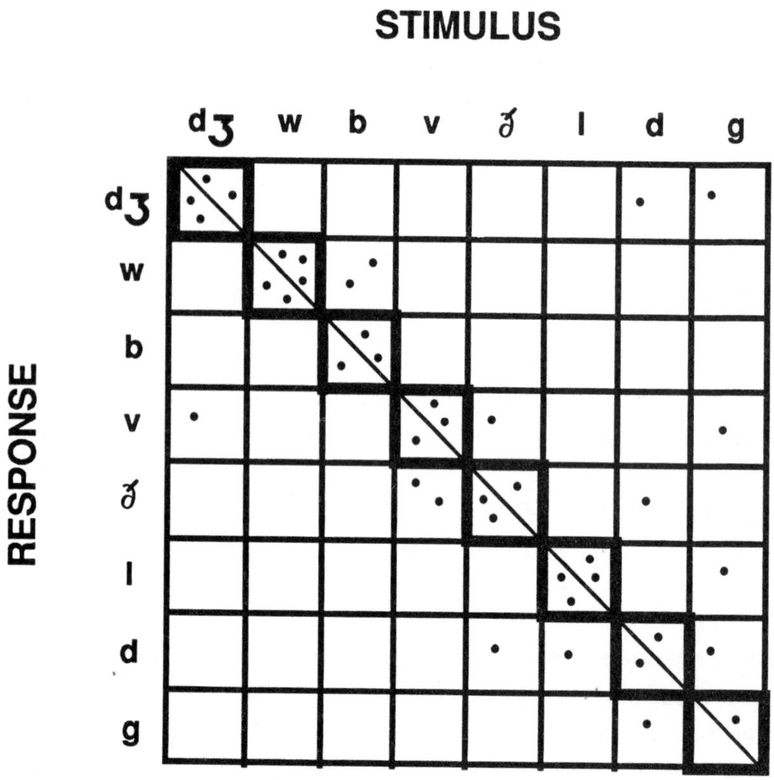

STIMULUS

Figure 3-2. A hearing-impaired adult's responses to LIST I (visual identification of consonants).

at least for this stimulus set, this syllable context, the illumination environment of the clinic, and the particular speaker who presented the test items.

Hearing-impaired adults have exhibited a range of response patterns (see Figure 3-2). Some error tendencies (e.g., /d/-/g/) are considered only minor aberrations, but others (e.g., /w/-/b/; /v/-/ð/) suggest the need for greater attention, perceptual practice, and/or additional visual assessment.

In addition, it has been interesting to note differences in clients' response latencies for the various visible stimuli. Hearing-impaired adults tend to identify frontal articulations (e.g., /dʒ ,w,b,v,ð/) more quickly and confidently. They usually identify less visible consonants (e.g., /d,g/) more slowly and with lower expressed confidence, and they often request repetitions of these items.

LIST II and LIST III: Screening Auditory Identification of Consonants

Many adults with acquired hearing losses are unable to reliably detect, discriminate, and/or identify particular spoken consonants by listening alone (Bailey, 1983). Sometimes, we are able to specify the client's auditory perception problem(s) when we observe persistent communication difficulties during simulated conversations, or when we examine the error patterns of an auditory word-identification test (e.g., responses to items from an AB Word List: Boothroyd, 1968). We often want to confirm these observations through more specific auditory screening.

The results of numerous research studies indicate that many hearing-impaired listeners are unable to reliably hear *place* of articulation in most consonants, and cannot hear *voicing* or *manner of articulation* in others (see Pickett, Martin, Johnson, Smith, Daniel, Willis, and Otis, 1972; Owens, Benedict, and Schubert, 1972; Sher and Owens, 1974; Walden and Montgomery, 1975). For example, many hearing-impaired people cannot clearly hear the qualitative differences between the pairs /p-t /, /m-n/, or /v-z/, when these consonants occur in spoken syllables. The misperceived distinguishing feature in each case - *place* of articulation - is very susceptible to the disruptive effects of hearing loss*, and hearing-impaired people commonly experience auditory errors of this type. Some acoustic confusions, however, are much less common. For example, only hearing-impaired people with very poor speech-perception ability consistently confuse the consonant pairs /t-d/, /m-b/, or/b-w/ as the distinguishing features here - voicing, nasality, and certain man-

---

* The place feature also is very susceptible to low-pass filtering, as well as to masking from background noise (see Miller and Nicely, 1955).

ner-of-articulation cues - are much more resistent to the disruptive effects of a sensorineural hearing disorder. Such research findings have led to the development of various auditory consonant-perception tests for clinical use, for example, the Nonsense Syllable Test (Danhauer, Garnett, and Edgerton, 1985). All of these tests have been valuable, and we acknowledge their use in the audiology clinic.

Our experience, however, has indicated that: (1) it takes a long time to administer a speech perception test that contains a large number of stimuli (with each item presented several times); (2) some hearing-impaired adults cannot store/recall a large set of response alternatives (even if a printed list is provided), and thus they may require numerous stimulus repetitions; (3) certain kinds of auditory errors are predictable in many forms of hearing impairment - that is, specific consonants are commonly confused with other consonants (e.g., members of the group of unvoiced fricatives /f, θ,ʃ, s/: see Walden, Montgomery, Prosek, and Schwartz, 1980); (4) consonant-test scores may not be correlated with the client's ability to engage in fluent auditory-visual (face-to-face) conversation in real life*, or with the client's "need" for hearing aids. For these reasons, we often screen auditory perception with a much smaller set of consonants, which are confused and mis-identified mainly by those with serious hearing impairments. That is, clients with minor auditory-perception problems have little difficulty with consonant identification; those who experience consistent and significant auditory distortions tend to perform poorly on these tests.

If we wish to obtain information about a hearing-impaired individual's ability to perceive *stop* and *nasal* consonants, we will present the set /p,t,k,b,d,g,m,n/ (i.e., LIST II). If we want to screen the

---

* Although the client may not be able to hear the differences between the voiceless fricative consonants /f,θ,ʃ, s/, he/she may be able to distinguish this group from other groups such as the voiced fricatives /v, ð, ʒ , z / or the voiceless stops /p, t, k/. If so, he/she should have little difficulty identifying /f/, /θ/, /ʃ/, or /s/ *audio-visually* in face-to-face conversation because: (a) they can be classified acoustically as voiceless fricatives; and (b) they differ greatly in their *visible* appearance.

STIMULUS

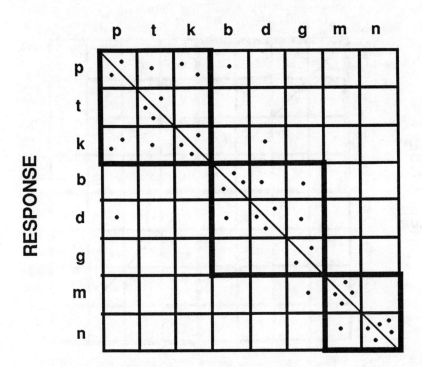

Figure 3-3. A hearing-impaired adult's responses to LIST II (auditory identification of stop and nasal consonants).

client's ability to identify the voiced/voiceless fricatives, we will present the set /f,θ,ʃ,s,v,ð,ʒ ,z/ (i.e., LIST III). These items are spoken in the intervocalic context /a/-C-/a/, five times each, in random order (40 total items). The test stimuli usually are presented under auditory conditions, but one also may present these sets visually and/or auditory-visually (see Erber, 1972). As the client identifies each spoken item, the response is recorded on an 8 x 8 matrix. Some typical results are illustrated in Figures 3-3 and 3-4.

STIMULUS

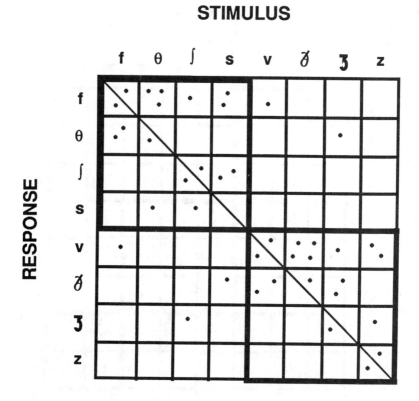

Figure 3-4. A hearing-impaired adult's responses to LIST III (auditory identification of fricative consonants)

A large number of auditory errors on LIST II or LIST III may suggest a need for analytical listening practice (e.g., discrimination, identification) during later sessions. We must recognize, however, that we cannot change a client's peripheral auditory system, which may be seriously limited in capacity. Hence, we may also need to show the client how to use lipreading or language-use strategies to compensate for the scarcity of usable acoustic information if the client does not know how to do this already.

Table 3-5. Lists of words containing high-frequency consonants (after Gardner, 1971)

kit	shipped	sips	sits	pick
sticks	fists	kissed	picked	thick
ticked	chicks	fist	sip	fixed
stiff	tips	skipped	fits	chips
fit	spit	kick	pitch	kiss
chip	fish	picks	chipped	sipped
fished	pit	spits	stick	ships
kicks	skip	tipped	kits	tip
sick	kicked	ship	fix	sit
pits	six	chick	tick	skips

Word Identification

To assess word identification, we may administer a conventional word list (e.g., a phonetically balanced list, such as PBs or NU-6) via auditory, visual, or auditory-visual modes. The test scores are expressed in terms of the proportion of words identified correctly under each condition. More often, however, we have used the AB (CVC) Word Lists (Boothroyd, 1968), where results are expressed in terms of the proportion of *phonemes* correctly identified. Specific consonant-identification errors that occur in word context (Table 1-1) may be compared with the results of testing with LIST II or LIST III.

We also have administered lists containing words loaded with high-frequency consonants (e.g., see Gardner, 1971) (Table 3-5). This test usually is presented via both auditory and auditory-visual modes, and the results in each case are compared. A comparison of the two scores frequently can be used to convince a skeptical client of his/her ability to use lipreading to complement impaired hearing. That is, someone with a high-frequency hearing loss may have great difficulty identifying the test words by listening alone (e.g., 2 out of 10 correct), but may be able to recognize nearly all of them when vision is permitted (e.g., 9 out of 10 correct).

Sentence Identification: SENT-IDENT

For assessing auditory, visual, or auditory-visual *sentence* identification, it is common to employ the CID Everyday Sentences (Davis and Silverman, 1978), where results are usually expressed in terms of key words identified correctly, or one may present items from the NAL Sentence Test (Plant and Macrae, 1981), where scores reflect the number of questions identified correctly. Each of these test strategies provides an estimate of the hearing-impaired individual's ability to perceive speech material that is longer than syllable or word length.

In these conventional approaches to perceptual assessment (for words or sentences), the test conditions typically are held constant (e.g., in quiet or in noise), each stimulus item is presented once, the hearing-impaired person's performance varies according to perceptual ability, and responses are scored in terms of "per cent correct". Thus, the testing procedures are reliable and "scientific", but they are quite unlike the events that occur during most human conversations, where the speaker may repeat several times and apply various forms of clarification to achieve intelligibility. In real life, the hearing-impaired person's degree of disability often is inferred from the amount of energy that the speaker must expend to communicate successfully (Erber, 1982).

We rarely employ conventional sentence-identification procedures in our clinic. Instead, when testing with sentences (e.g., see Table 3-6), we now present each item several times, modifying the stimulus each time to compensate for the client's previous (error) responses. That is, we repeatedly present each sentence, requiring an identification response each time, until the client eventually identifies 100% of its content. These successive presentations, however, are given under different stimulus conditions, according to a hierarchy: (1) the sentence is spoken *initially without acoustic cues**; (2) the sentence is *repeated* without acoustic cues; (3)

---

* These stimulus conditions may be reversed for particular clients. That is, sentences in Conditions #1, 2, and 3 are presented with *acoustic* cues alone (i.e., mouth covered), and key words/phrases in Condition #4 are presented with the mouth briefly *uncovered*. A similar procedure is commonly used by teachers of hearing-impaired children during "auditory training" (see Erber, 1982).

Table 3-6. Examples of sentences used in the SENT-IDENT assessment procedure.

If you don't hurry, we're going to be late.
My new black shirt is missing a button.
Next year, we're going on a holiday cruise.
Where can I buy a pair of green shoelaces?
Two aspirins will cure your headache.
He said that yellow was his favourite colour.
His dog tore a hole in my new rug.
After I finish this report, I'm going home.
My neighbour's cat likes to sleep under the car.
Would you mind turning the music down a little?
This town's so small, it's not even on the map.
She stared at the wedding gown in the window.
He couldn't get the spot out of his coat.
The plumber installed the shower on Tuesday.
You aren't allowed to smoke in this office.
The cake is beautiful, but it's too sweet.
The taxi driver shook his fist as the truck went by.
The children made funny faces at the monkeys.
We carried our suitcases out to the plane.
A large crowd of people gathered at the corner.

---

the sentence is *repeated with increased clarity* (appropriate stress, pause, elongation, and so forth), again without acoustic cues; (4) the sentence is *repeated with acoustic cues added* - for selected key words or phrases; (5) the *entire sentence is presented via audition and vision.* This procedure (SENT-IDENT) is based partly on assessment or remediation techniques suggested by Erber and DeFilippo (1978), Hull (1976,1982), and Owens and Telleen (1981).

To summarize the results, we note the stimulus condition under which each test sentence was identified correctly. "Scores" are expressed as the number of times that each stimulus condition was required by the hearing-impaired client to correctly identify a set of sentences (see Table

Table 3-7. SENT-IDENT results. Twenty sentences (see Table 3-6) were presented to a severely hearing-impaired client (O.R., female, age 72 years) for identification under various visual and auditory-visual conditions. As prescribed by the SENT-IDENT procedure (see pp. 70-72), available perceptual information was increased throughout five successive live-voice presentations of each sentence. Scores are summarized below.

	Number of Sentences Identified Correctly
Visible cues alone (original presentation)	0
Visible cues alone (simple repetition)	1
Visible cues alone (exaggerated repetition)	2
Visible cues, plus voiced key word only	5
Acoustic and visible cues: entire sentence	12
Total	20

3-7). In this approach to assessment of communication skills, the level of receptive performance is held constant (at 100%), and the testing conditions are varied - to discover which modifications in the stimulus sentences are necessary to help the client achieve this score. Specifying the minimal auditory and visual conditions which the client requires to identify sentences can be very useful to the clinician in planning the perceptual environment for later communication therapy. This adaptive approach to testing is similar to that used in the Tracking Procedure (see pp. 95-99) (DeFilippo and Scott, 1978; Owens and Telleen, 1981) and also in Subtest 3 of the GASP! (see Erber, 1982).

QUEST?AR Evaluation Two (QE II)

Hearing-impaired people can recognize words more easily when the words occur in redundant sentences (e.g., "This key won't fit in the *lock*.") than when they are spoken in non-predictive sentences (e.g., "He didn't know anything about the *lock*.") (Kalikow, Stevens, and Elliott, 1977). In addition, a hearing-impaired person's ability to identify a spoken word or sentence can be affected by the environmental or situational context (Garstecki and O'Neill, 1980). Our clinical experiences suggest that one's ability to identify a word or sentence also is strongly influenced by the position of the item in a conversational interchange, that is, by *pragmatic* factors as well. Accordingly, one can intentionally present stimulus words or sentences in *interactive* contexts and thereby examine the effects of pragmatic factors on their intelligibility. The results may be closely related to the hearing-impaired person's (auditory, visual, or auditory-visual) word- and sentence-identification performance in real conversations (see Erber, 1985).

In most conventional test procedures, the client simply attends passively as each stimulus item is presented (clinician presents stimulus item > client responds). In this proposed variation on clinical assessment, the client asks a prepared question (e.g., reading from a printed list), and the clinician answers the question by presenting the corresponding stimulus word or sentence (client asks question > clinician presents stimulus item > client responds). Some examples are given in Table 3-8. The process is very similar to that employed in the ASQUE>>> procedure described later in this text (see pp. 129-138).

The clinician can present matched sets of words or sentences under several pragmatic conditions (types of "conversational" context), and then can compare the results. For example, in the QE II procedure, these questions may be: (1) non-limiting - the client simply asks, "What is the next sentence?"; (2) moderately predictive - the client asks, "What did you see at the corner?"; or (3) highly predictive - the client asks, "Why did the truck stop so suddenly?". The clinician's stimulus sentence in each case would be: "Two old men were crossing the street." The hearing-impaired client's ability to identify that sentence may vary considerably according to the predictive nature of his/her question that preceded it.

If a hearing-impaired client can easily identify a set of stimulus sentences when they are spoken *without* predictive context, then there is high potential for success in ordinary conversation, even if the other

Table 3-8. Application of the QE II question-answer test procedure to presentation of a group of CID Everyday Sentences (Davis and Silverman, 1978) (after Erber, 1985). a. no context; b. limiting context.

Client's Question	Clinician's Answer (stimulus sentence)
a.	
"What did you say?"	(any sentence)
b.	
"Why did you come back?"	"The water's too cold for swimming."
"What do you like to do?"	"Walking's my favourite exercise."
"Could you help me, please?"	"I'll carry the package for you."
"What would you like to eat?"	"Pass the bread and butter please."
"What's happening outside?"	"It's raining."
"Why did you stop working?"	"There isn't enough paint to finish the room."
"Why aren't you coming with us?"	"I don't want to go to the movies tonight."
"Why is everyone leaving?"	"The show's over."
"How will I get home?"	"You can catch the bus across the street."

communicator frequently changes the topic. But if the client can obtain understanding only when words are spoken in *redundant sentences* (see Kalikow, Stevens, and Elliott, 1977), or only when spoken sentences are given in response to *predictive questions* (e.g., QE II above), then that hearing-impaired individual may need to learn how to consciously select topics and guide the format of conversations to obtain an acceptable degree of fluency.

EXAMINING CONVERSATIONAL ABILITIES: TOPICON

Description / Procedures

TOPICON is a simple conversation-sampling, evaluation, and practice procedure which we have developed for clinical use (see Table 3-9). Conversations may be elicited from hearing-impaired clients on a wide range of topics (see Davis and Wilcox, 1985).

The four main components of the procedure are: (1) each communicator (client, clinician) indicates topics in which he/she has interest and about which he/she has knowledge; (2) one participant selects a topic for conversation from these lists - reflecting his/her own knowledge and experience, that of the communication partner, or both; (3) the two participants conduct a brief conversation about the chosen topic, during which the clinician monitors and assesses events; (4) the client and the clinician discuss the contents and fluency of the conversation, considering avoidance or resolution of communication difficulties (see Table 3-9).

As the hearing-impaired client marks preferred topics (see Table 3-10), he/she may become aware that people differ, and thus exhibit dissimilar fields of knowledge and interest. The client also may discover (by reference to the clinician's selections) that his/her own personal choices reflect a relatively broad/narrow scope of potential topics for conversation.

If the *client* is permitted to choose the topic, he/she has four general options, typical of all conversations. The hearing-impaired person may: (1) select a conversational topic which both participants have marked (a common occurrence); thus both are familiar with the topic and express interest in it; (2) choose a topic that is interesting only to him/herself (a slightly less common event); (3) choose a topic that is personally unfamiliar, but one that is of interest to the clinician (an uncommon choice); or (4) select a topic for conversation that is unknown or is of little interest to either participant (a rare occurrence). If the *clinician* assumes control of this preliminary decision and selects the topic, then of course any combination of relative interests and knowledge may be selected, and the choice of topic can be made in a deliberate manner to demonstrate the resulting effects on communication.

Table 3-9. General instructions for TOPICON, a simple conversation sampling, evaluation, and practice procedure.

---

1. Give one list of conversation topics to the client, and give another list to his/her communication partner (e.g., the clinician) (Table 3-10).

2. The client and the communication partner each indicate (circle) familiar topics on the list. Each person marks topics that he/she considers interesting and likes to talk about. Then the two participants compare and discuss their choices.

3. The clinician (or client) selects a topic for conversation - reflecting the client's interest and/or that of the communication partner.

4. The client and the communication partner conduct a brief conversation on the chosen topic for 5 to 10 minutes. Background noise, visual distractions, and/or speech and language difficulties may be introduced during the conversation.

5. Then, the clinician and the client discuss what happened during the conversation, for example:

    a. What are the advantages/disadvantages of discussing a familiar/unfamiliar topic?
    b. What happens when neither person knows very much about the topic?
    c. Who talked more during the conversation? Why?
    d. Who asked more questions/gave more answers? Why?
    e. What was the general direction of "information flow": to/from the client?
    f. Which factors resulted in fluency/disruption during the conversation?
    g. Which clarification strategies were applied (in)effectively?

6. The clinician and/or observers may assess various characteristics of the (videotaped) conversation: e.g., "fluency" and related factors (Tables 3-11, 3-12).

Choosing a topic for conversation on the basis of mutual interest and knowledge, unbalanced interest, or mutual disinterest tends to strongly affect the general direction of information flow to or from the client, as

Table 3-10. The list of topics which is used to elicit conversation from a hearing-impaired adult during the TOPICON procedure (see pp. 75-85).

house renovation	electronics	writing poetry
dancing	cave exploring	antique furniture
types of cheese	barbecues	close friend
gossip	cats	newspaper ads
space travel	swimming	beer
computers	best recipes	going fishing
bicycle racing	gardening	jewellery
going shopping	tennis	last weekend
astrology	saving money	babies
television	sailing	recent illness
new clothes	stamp collecting	old movies
restaurants	raising pigs	the weather
mountain climbing	the theatre	going to work
car repair	politics	camping
books	family parties	dogs
today's news	at the beach	holidays
cigarette smoking	supermarkets	mowing the lawn
national parks	growing mushrooms	wine
knitting	new shoes	roof repair
vitamins	train travel	favourite foods

well as the nature of the interaction (see Figure 3-5). The choice of topic thus can strongly affect the developing sequence of statements, questions, and answers within the conversation. It is likely that the person who knows least about the conversational topic will ask the most questions, attempting to find out more from the other communicator, who usually will provide most of the information. The conversation may follow an orderly question-answer format, with recognizable contingent (or "adjacency") pairs (Clark and Clark, 1977; DiMatteo and DiNicola, 1982).

When *both* communicators know quite a bit about the chosen topic, the organization of the conversation may be somewhat less orderly. Many

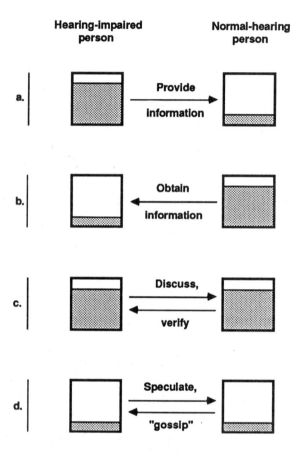

Figure 3-5. Information balance and general direction of flow in conversations. Shading indicates the amount of information that each communicator possesses about the topic (after Erber, 1985).

more assertions may occur, as well as narrative, and interruptions may be more frequent, as each participant attempts to gain control of the conversation and present his/her own experiences, information, ideas, and opinions. Conversations on topics of *little* interest to both communicators are likely to end quickly, unless the two people mutually agree (not) to change the topic and continue.

A conversation between a person with normal hearing and a person with a serious hearing impairment may be atypical in several specific ways. For example, a particular conversation may be characterized by numerous gaps, re-starts, diversions, topic shifts, meta-communication episodes, disruptions in turn-taking, superficiality, lack of abstraction, extreme self-consciousness, incomplete understanding, and so forth (Table 1-2). These factors tend to reduce the rate of exchange of information and thus the degree of conversational fluency. Consequently, both clients and clinicians usually work to eliminate these impediments during subsequent communication therapy.

It can be especially interesting to note and examine the underlying factors that seem to contribute to breakdowns in conversation. These may include the use of rare words, colloquial expressions, or complex sentence structures by the communication partner, the application of non-specific clarification strategies by the hearing-impaired client (such as "What?", "Pardon?", "Sorry?"), client-dominated conversation, or instances where the client abruptly alters the flow of the conversation to coincide with his/her own interests - often as the result of communication failure. In order to maintain naturalness and objectivity, the clinician refrains from discussing these factors *during* the TOPICON activity (Davis and Wilcox, 1985).

Numerous checklists or rating scales have been used to qualitatively describe the nature of simulated conversations (see Bedrosian, 1985; Davis and Wilcox, 1985; Prutting and Kirchner, 1987). For example, a clinician may rate: "naturalness", "style", "continuity", "topic maintenance", and so forth. Or, one may even count or measure: the proportion of communication problems identified correctly; the turns-per-minute rate; the proportion of total time used by each talker; or the proportion of time used for information exchange. To assess TOPICON sessions, we have chosen to rate overall "fluency" and also fifteen related pragmatic factors (Table 3-11). Clinicians report that it is relatively easy to apply these scales to describe a conversation, once the various linguistic terms are understood (see definitions: Table 3-12).

Table 3-11. Form used for assessing "fluency" of TOPICON sessions and other conversations (see Prutting and Kirchner, 1987). Results are shown for a "simulated" conversation between a hearing-impaired adult and her clinician.

Topic: _Shopping_

Topic familiarity:

	Clinician Low	High
Client Low	☐	☐
Client High	☐	☑

Overall "fluency" of discourse:

Low				High
__	✔	__	__	__

Factors related to fluency:

	Low				High
a. presupposition	__	__	__	✔	__
b. receptive abilities (A,V, A-V)	✔	__	__	__	__
c. expressive abilities	__	__	__	✔	__
d. motivation, attention	__	__	__	__	✔
e. turntaking	__	✔	__	__	__
f. specificity/accuracy	__	__	__	__	✔
g. *new* vs *old* information	__	__	__	__	✔
h. non-verbal communication	__	✔	__	__	__
i. topic maintenance	__	__	__	✔	__
j. cooperation	__	__	__	__	✔
k. time-sharing	✔	__	__	__	__
l. verification	__	✔	__	__	__
m. independent repair	✔	__	__	__	__
n. meta-communication	__	__	✔	__	__
o. other _____	__	__	__	__	__

Comments:
withdraws from conversation; avoids use of repair strategies; submissive; bluffs when unsure.

The TOPICON session itself, its assessment, as well as the discussion between the client and clinician that follows, all provide clues regarding directions to take during subsequent therapy sessions. For example, the client may need to learn socially acceptable ways for redirecting the topic. He/she may need guidance in how to maintain a conversation whose content is unfamiliar. The client may need help in selecting and applying appropriate clarification strategies.

TOPICON with Auditory and Visual Distractions
As previously stated, hearing-impaired people frequently experience difficulty in group discussions, or in places where excessive noise is present (e.g., at a business meeting, in an airline terminal, in a restaurant). They report that these communication environments are major sources of conversational dysfluency. To help our clients manage in these situations, we need to fully appreciate the nature and degree of their communication difficulties - that is, we need to observe them attempting to communicate in such situations. The clinician may be misled if assessments are carried out only in quiet, non-distracting environments (Garstecki and O'Neill, 1980; Garstecki, 1981a; Davis and Wilcox, 1985).

Many of our hearing-impaired clients indicate that they commonly find themselves engaged in a face-to-face (auditory-visual) conversation during which fluctuations in background noise level and in noise quality obscure numerous relevant acoustic cues for speech. Without warning, excessive noise may force them to suddenly shift to the *visual-only* mode for message reception. Later, when the acoustic disruption has passed, they are able to return to the auditory-visual mode. Conversely, they may be forced to shift suddenly to the *auditory-only* mode of perception if the talker turns away and thus breaks visual contact, or if other unwanted visible distractions intrude (e.g., someone walks between the communicators).

We often carry out TOPICON evaluation and practice sessions in noisy and/or visually distracting environments which closely match those designated as "difficult" by the hearing-impaired client. For example, during a simulated conversation, we may play audio record-

Table 3-12. Guide to assessing fluency of TOPICON and other conversations: definition of terms.

---

* **fluency** - an attribute of a conversation in which information, ideas, feelings, and attitudes are exchanged in an efficient and coherent manner; such a conversation contains few diversions, little explanation or self-clarification, and not very much meta-communication.

Related factors:

a. **presupposition** - client correctly judges his/her communication partner's status, age, sex, degree of authority, level of knowledge, attitudes, feelings, amount of detail desired, and willingness to participate in the conversation.

b. **receptive abilities** - client is able to extract maximal speech/language information through (aided) auditory, (aided) vibro-tactile, and visual modalities.

c. **expressive abilities** - client speaks clearly with intelligibility; is able to provide maximal speech/language information at a normal rate; uses language that is semantically and syntactically correct.

d. **motivation, attention** - client exhibits a healthy state, a high level of concentration, a positive attitude toward communication, an absence of fatigue; is neither preoccupied nor distracted.

e. **turntaking** - client exhibits appropriate interactive timing; avoids abnormally long silent intervals as well as overlaps/interruptions.

f. **specificity** - client is careful and precise in use of language; consistently names referents; is not ambiguous or vague (e.g., does not say, "They put the other things somewhere!").

g. **new vs old information** - client consistently introduces new ideas and experiences; avoids presenting information, ideas, and feelings previously discussed - both within and between conversations.

h. **non-verbal communication** - client uses facial expression, gesture, posture, eye contact, proximity, and physical contact appropriately and in a manner that matches his/her communicative intent.

Table 3-12. continued

---

i. **topic maintenance** - client maintains topic cohesion for an appropriate time - until information is exhausted or becomes repetitious; client shifts, and returns to, topics in a socially acceptable manner (e.g., does not say, "I'm bored .....").

j. **cooperation** - client participates with authenticity and honesty; client confronts all issues and interaction without excessive role-playing, joking, bluffing, or pretense.

k. **time-sharing** - client is neither excessively dominant/controlling nor submissive/withdrawn in conversation; takes an appropriate share of time to present his/her information, ideas, or feelings (not too much or too little).

l. **verification** - client periodically informs his/her communication partner how messages were received, and also determines that the communication partner has accurately received his/her expressed messages.

m. **independent repair** - client assumes principal responsibility for clarification of conversational difficulties or resolution of communication breakdown; identifies problems accurately and applies strategies appropriately.

n. **meta-communication** - client demonstrates language awareness; is able to observe, analyse, and discuss his/her own language acts (e.g., can answer questions, such as: "Why do you think that last sentence was easy/difficult for you to understand?" and "Why do you think he/she is still interested in that topic?").

o. **other** - (insert any additional factor that seems to contribute to, or detract from, conversational fluency, efficiency, or naturalness; then rate its contribution).

*** Note: Because all conversations are *interactive*, with each person influenced by and responding to the other's verbal/non-verbal acts, the communication partner's utterances or behaviours may stimulate the emergence/emphasis of particular behaviours in the client. Thus, the contributions of the communication partner (e.g., clinician, friend, family member) and the relationship between the communicators also must be carefully observed and noted.

---

ings selected from our tape library of noise backgrounds (e.g., busy street corner, building construction, restaurant, commuter train, supermarket). Alternatively, we may use a sample of noise previously recorded by the client at home or at work (e.g., dinner time, television, back yard, office) - to establish a typically disruptive environment for assessment or for communication practice. We may even invite students, clinicians, and/or other staff members to provide their physical presence as well as their voice babble, to create realism during these sessions*.

We use a trial-and-error approach to modify the environment of the clinic room until the hearing-impaired client claims that the amount and type of noise, reverberation, visual distraction, number of people present, and so forth approximates a typical "problem" situation. Then, under these agreed-upon conditions, we conduct simulated conversations.

During all TOPICON sessions, we observe any minor difficulties or breakdowns in conversation that occur, we note all remedial strategies applied (or disregarded) by the hearing-impaired client, and we consider the appropriateness and effectiveness of these techniques (see pp. 117-124). We also may *intentionally* create communication difficulties (e.g., speak too rapidly, reduce voice level, obscure mouth) to cause conversational dysfluencies, to stimulate assertiveness in the client, and to encourage the use of a range of clarification requests (see Table 4-12). Our overall purpose is to examine the client's ability to successfully manage a conversation under realistic and difficult conditions.

---

* We, as well as most of our hearing-impaired clients, find that conversational situations enacted with *fluctuating* distraction are much more realistic (and are much more disruptive to conversation) than are those created by presenting a background of steady-state, electronically generated masking noise (e.g., "pink" or "white") or even recorded voice babble.

SUMMARY

Intake and assessment procedures can be efficient, effective, and relevant clinical tools. Many of the tests presented here are new, created especially for the communication therapy programme introduced in this text. Many are non-traditional. Some are conversation-based, rather than perceptual in nature. We have chosen to describe these procedures because we have found them to be brief, realistic, and practical for use with most adults who have acquired hearing impairments. Moreover, the results of each assessment suggest particular directions for subsequent communication therapy.

4

COMMUNICATION PRACTICE

COMMON CONVERSATIONAL OCCURRENCES

Some hearing-impaired people misperceive parts of every conversation in which they participate. These misunderstandings may occur because of the length and complexity of the messages, the speaker's (lack of) clarity, environmental distractions, modifications to the speech signal by hearing aid(s), or auditory distortions. A spoken message may be perceived by a hearing-impaired person in many different ways (Table 4-1).

For example, at any particular time during a conversation, a hearing-impaired person may perceive a message that is expected and "makes sense" (e.g., "Last Friday, we ate dinner at my brother's house."). That is, the message may answer a question that previously was asked, it may fit into a list of items that are being described, or it may topically and logically follow the preceding sentences in a narrative. In this case, we presume that the hearing-impaired person has perceived what his/her communication partner actually said, and that correct perception (message identification and comprehension) has occurred.

Table 4-1. Conversational occurrences. Hearing-impaired people report many types of perceptual experiences.

---

1. **Perceived a message correctly** - received a meaningful message that was expected and pragmatically appropriate [e.g., "Where's the main post office?" - *"Two blocks down, and turn right."*].

2. **Perceived an incorrect meaningful message** - received a message that fit the conversation, but one that represented incorrect perception nevertheless [e.g., re bad apples: *"They're not good for anything but chucking!"* (actually, "chutney")].

3. **Perceived a meaningless message confidently** - perceived a message clearly, but one that did not make sense and did not fit the conversation [e.g., "Didn't she understand?" "No. *I explained it in my typical Garibaldi faction."* (actually, "...typically garbled fashion")].

4. **Perceived nonsense** - received a series of syllables and word-like patterns, but could not understand them [e.g., "Did you get all your work finished?" - *"Mau fitr pekd laimmi aruipeng!"*].

5. **Perceived fragments** - received only part of the message, perhaps incorrectly [e.g., "Why didn't you buy the tape recorder?" - *"Because we saw..in the shop window."*].

6. **Perceived (distorted) acoustic cues only** - the speaker's mouth was not visible (e.g., as over the telephone; or his/her mouth was obscured by hair, a hand, or an object).

7. **Perceived (incomplete) visible cues only** - the speaker was too far away; the speaker's voice level was too low; the hearing aids and/or batteries were malfunctioning.

8. **Perceived nothing** - the receiver was distracted or was not paying attention, so the speaker's utterance was neither heard nor seen.

There may be another instance, however, where the hearing-impaired person confidently perceives a similar spoken message which seems to fit the conversational context, but this time, the message is received *incorrectly* (e.g., "Next Sunday, we're going to see an old Betty Grable movie at the Astor Theatre"). Sometimes, closer attention resolves the perceptual confusion* when/if the utterance is repeated, but often the speaker must consciously apply a clarification strategy, such as rephrasing, or providing more information. Sometimes this type of perceptual error may not become apparent to either communicator until later in the conversation, or even long after the conversation has ended - when the hearing-impaired person responds to the information or request incorrectly (see Table 4-2).

Where the spoken message is received with high confidence, but the words do not convey meaning in the framework of the conversation (e.g., "They lived in *Leg Force*......"), the hearing-impaired communicator probably will suspect that part of the utterance has been misperceived. If so, one can work to repair the conversation by requesting/applying certain clarification strategies (e.g., "They lived where...?"). In other instances, the hearing-impaired person will be *certain* that he/she has misperceived the message, because virtually none of it is intelligible (e.g., "Idth uh roke...in bay mid-day......chah ku"). Here, the hearing-impaired communicator and the normal-hearing communication partner must work together to carefully modify the content and form of the intended message. Their shared goal is to re-shape the utterance, fitting it into the hearing-impaired person's range of perceptual and linguistic abilities (Davis and Wilcox, 1985).

Upon receiving an unclear or ambiguous message, many hearing-impaired people attempt *pragmatic* strategies first (see pp. 109-116). That is, given the topic and recent content of the conversation and also the specific nature of the preceeding utterance, a person frequently can successfully "guess" how the communication partner might have responded. This approach can fail, however, and the hearing-impaired communicator may then need to examine any patterns remaining in auditory or visual short-term memory, using knowledge of language (word order, word associations, accumulated experience with previous conversations) to re-construct the message. There are times, however, when the hearing-impaired communicator may be unable to apply even

---

* In this instance, *Greta Garbo* was misperceived as *Betty Grable*.

Table 4-2. Some unusual confusions that occurred during a conversation before a meal. This interchange resulted from a sequence of ambiguous events and perceptual errors. Each communicator was misdirected by the context that he/she presupposed (see Watzlawick, Bavelas, and Jackson (1967) for a similar example).

The situation: A man (M) and a woman (F) are eating some bread and butter. The man finishes eating first. The woman gets two glasses and casually places them on the table.

The conversation:

(as the <u>woman</u> perceived it)	(as the <u>man</u> perceived it)
F: "Would you like some wine?"	F: "Would you like some more?"
M: "Red?"	M: "Bread?"
F: "No, white!"	F: "No, white!"
M: "What?"	M: "What?"
F: "I've already opened the *white!*"	F: "I've already opened the *white!*"
M: "I know! We've just been eating it!"	M: "I know! We've just been eating it!"
F: "What?"	F: "What?"
....	....

The explanation:

At this point in the conversation, both F and M resorted to meta-communication to discover the source(s) of their respective confusions. They discovered that: F had perceived *bread* as *red*; M had perceived *wine* as *more*.

---

these latent linguistic skills successfully. If so, one must resort to conscious perceptual analysis of (numerous repetitions of) any available sensory information (e.g., prosody, phonemes, visemes) in the spoken message to ultimately establish its identity. This sequence of receptive strategies may be referred to as "top-down" language processing (Ling and Nienhuys, 1983; Lubinsky, 1986).

PERCEPTUAL PRACTICE

During a series of rehabilitation sessions, we often find that our hearing-impaired clients already seem to be performing many speech-communication tasks at an optimal *perceptual* level. They may have learned how to identify ambiguous auditory and visual speech stimuli as a result of long-term experience in receiving speech through their own imperfect sensory systems. If this is the case, specific perceptual/analytical practice may not be necessary or recommended.

Occasionally, however, screening test results suggest that an adult hearing-impaired client might benefit from a short course of directed perceptual (re-)learning. Some people show rapid improvement in identification of ambiguous stimulus items once the distinctive audible or visible elements of speech are pointed out to them (Walden, Erdman, Montgomery, Schwartz, and Prosek, 1981), but others do not learn so quickly. It is important for these latter clients to recognize that they do in fact have perceptual limitations, that we can specify these limitations (e.g., an inability to hear or see the differences between /si/ and /t i/), and that they cannot easily eliminate their perceptual difficulties as the result of concentrated listening or lipreading practice.

When perceptual practice *is* recommended, it usually involves helping the client to visually recognize small dimensional or articulatory differences between similar mouth configurations, or to distinguish between imprecisely heard sound qualities (e.g., "features") that denote particular groups of acoustic speech units. Hearing-impaired adults differ in the extent to which they are able to extract such detailed visible or acoustic information from speech. Therefore, they also will differ in the degree to which they will benefit from perceptual/analytical practice and consciously increased attention to fine detail in the spoken message.

Lipreading

During initial lipreading screening, a particular hearing-impaired client may consistently make consonant or vowel identification errors which are not *typical** . Some examples are: persistent visual confusion between /l/ and /d/, between /v/ and /ð/, or perhaps between /I/ and /U/. Comparable errors may frequently occur during simulated conversations also, but these ongoing substitutions may not be so prominent or consistent as in screening test results because of contextual effects which can obscure many *perceptual* difficulties.

More detailed visual/lipreading assessment and perceptual (analytical) practice may be carried out**. The presumed basis of the perceptual error in each instance above is identified and demonstrated: /l/-/d/ (both are produced with the tongue tip visible, forward, and raised to the palate); /v/-/ð/ (both involve visible upper front teeth as prominent articulators); /I/-/U/ (both have similar vertical mouth opening). The clinician may refer to his/her own mouth as a model of exemplary visible articulation, or one may point out the distinguishing visible features in photos, slides, stop-frame films, or videotapes (Franks, 1976). The client may articulate the confused pairs himself/herself and thereby appreciate the relevant differences through proprioceptive feedback (Bunger, 1961).

The hearing-impaired client also may be given a brief series of perceptual exercises in which direct comparisons are made between the confused items. Here, he/she carefully observes and attempts to recognize the distinctive articulatory cues for the pair /l/-/d/ (tongue pointing vs spreading), for /v/-/ð/ (upper teeth touching lower lip vs tongue touching upper teeth), or the visible cues for /I/-/U/ (slightly spread vs slightly narrowed horizontal lip aperture).

---

* *Typical* lipreading errors include confusions within the groups /p, b, m/, /f, v/, /t, d, n, s, z, (k, g)/, and so forth. (Jeffers and Barley, 1971).

** Most of these teaching procedures employ the following approach: the clinician presents a stimulus item; the client repeats/points/writes what was spoken; the clinician provides feedback regarding the correctness of the response; the clinician or the client applies/requests a clarification strategy (e.g., articulatory exaggeration); the clinician presents the stimulus item again; the client responds again; etc. Later, both discuss the reasons for the client's success or difficulty in perceiving the spoken stimulus correctly.

Same-different *discrimination* tasks in syllable context may be combined with single-stimulus (i.e., forced-choice response) *identification* tasks - where immediate feedback is given after each response (Walden, Prosek, Montgomery, Scherr, and Jones, 1977; Walden, Erdman, Montgomery, Schwartz, and Prosek, 1981). Later, contrasting words incorporating the potentially confusing articulations may be presented for identification - in isolation and in phrase/sentence context.

The clinician also may demonstrate how the surrounding vowel or consonant environment can modify or even obscure the distinctive visible features of speech articulation and thus can seriously confound one's ability to recognize them through lipreading. For example, /l/ is not an alveolar consonant before /k/, as in the word *milk*. Neither /l/ nor /d/ can be reliably identified in /u/-/C/-/u/ context, as in the words *zulu* or *voodoo*. And, when /U/ follows /ʃ/, as in the word *shook*, it becomes indistinct to the lipreader.

Listening

When we feel that a hearing-impaired client can benefit from listening practice, we usually follow a therapy programme like that prescribed by Erber (1982). Our model for therapy is based to an extent on auditory training methods devised by Urbantschitsch (1895), and later expanded by Goldstein (1939), and Carhart (1961). We, however, recognize that: (1) the physiology of one's impaired auditory system (at least peripherally) cannot be changed by a series of planned listening exercises; (2) analytical listening practice may be uninteresting to many hearing-impaired adults (and also to their clinicians); (3) most people with gradually acquired hearing losses already have gained quite a bit of valuable experience listening through their impaired ears, and so they have previously developed a range of special perceptual abilities. Moreover, some clinicians feel that it is inappropriate to devote much time to rehabilitation of the *impaired* sense, and instead suggest that one's efforts be directed to teaching the hearing-impaired client *compensatory* skills (e.g., lipreading, or communication strategies).

In our clinical experience, however, guided listening practice can be of benefit to many hearing-impaired adults (Rubenstein and Boothroyd, 1987). This is especially true for those who have recently obtained (their own or trial) hearing aids and are now receiving amplified sounds which they cannot easily identify*. The new hearing aids make numerous sounds more audible than before. Some people, however, have not perceived particular sound qualities for many years, and so they cannot remember their significance. Some speech sounds (e.g., /ʃ/) may assume new acoustic prominence in received verbal messages, where vision previously had been used as the primary compensatory mode. Other speech sounds (e.g., /s/) may sound strange or unpleasant, relative to the way that they previously were heard.

Numerous environmental sounds which are newly audible may not be recognized reliably (e.g., water running). Other amplified sounds may be annoying (e.g., traffic noise) or even frightening (e.g., a door slamming, or a dog barking). A new hearing aid user can gain familiarity and learn to cope with each of these sound situations during guided listening practice.

In the auditory training programme suggested by Erber (1982), speech stimuli (e.g., phonemes, words, sentences) and response levels (e.g., detection, identification, comprehension) form hierarchies. These are depicted in a two-dimensional matrix (Figure 1-3), where the intersection of each stimulus and response defines a listening activity of particular difficulty. *Sentences* are presumed to be more difficult to hear accurately than *words* because of their greater length and complexity (although the positive contributions of linguistic context are recognized). *Comprehension* is presumed to be more difficult than *detection* because of the memory and association processes required. An adaptive procedure is recommended, by which the clinician selects, devises, and administers listening activities.

The listener's response tendencies are noted. If a given listening task

---

* This experience is especially common among profoundly hearing-impaired people who recently have received a cochlear implant and who are being introduced to a wide variety of auditory sensations without obvious (visual, tactual) associations or referents to their source (Eisenberg, 1985).

consistently yields auditory *success*, then another task employing more complex speech stimuli and/or higher levels of response are indicated. If perceptual *difficulties* are consistently encountered, then less complex stimuli and/or response levels are suggested (see Figure 1-3). The resulting adaptive shifts in task complexity tend to lead to appropriate challenges and rewards for both the client and the clinician.

Tracking Procedure

The evaluation and practice procedure known as "Tracking" (DeFilippo and Scott, 1978) can easily be employed as an auditory and/or visual activity. Tracking is an *identification* procedure - the speaker presents a portion of speech material, the client repeats whatever part of the message has been received, and the speaker responds as necessary to ensure correct message reception. *Comprehension* (understanding) of the message is not necessarily examined, although this can be assessed if desired. Tracking originally was developed to evaluate lipreading performance (see Danz and Binnie, 1983) and also to estimate the potential benefit of various lipreading aids, but the same general procedure has been used, with minor modifications, for both auditory assessment and training (Owens and Telleen, 1981; Owens and Raggio, 1987) and for providing auditory practice to hearing-impaired people listening over the telephone (Erber, 1982, 1985).

The method can be applied in the following way for auditory and/or visual communication practice. After preliminary introduction of the task procedure and unambiguous face-to-face practice with "easy" text material, the clinician and the client are ready to begin. The clinician reads portions of a novel, short story, or newspaper article* to the

---

* This sort of practice typically has been applied with narrative (text: e.g., newspaper articles, short stories, novels), each segment containing about 200-500 words to be completed per session. The Tracking Procedure, however, also may be applied with prepared *lists* - of names (people, streets, cities), numbers (telephone numbers, addresses, prices), objects (furniture, tools, clothing, foods), and so forth. In such instances, as before, correct repetition is required for each item, remedial strategies are applied as needed, and the sessions are timed.

hearing-impaired person. The client looks and/or listens carefully via sensory aids and attempts to repeat (identify) word-for-word what was said - as quickly as possible. The clinician presents the material in segments whose lengths (entire sentences, phrases, words, or syllables) depend on the ease with which the hearing-impaired client seems to be receiving spoken messages at that particular time.

If the client's response is not an exact repetition of the stimulus, then the clinician is expected to apply a potentially effective remedial strategy to help that person repeat the message more accurately. For example, one may try presenting the message segment again, perhaps breaking it into brief phrases (or even single words, if necessary). One may try presenting the message word-by-word, exaggerating articulation (e.g., increase voice level, insert pauses, decrease speech rate, stress weak syllables, elongate vowel duration). Or, one may substitute synonyms, vary syntax, or spell by means of a pre-arranged code (see Erber and Greer, 1973; Castle, 1980; Erber, 1982; Owens and Telleen, 1981).

The purpose for this work is to help the hearing-impaired person ultimately receive (and repeat) all segments of a message perfectly. The *clinician* may choose the remedial strategy to apply when difficulty occurs, but it is now apparent that this form of speech- communication practice has the greatest long-term benefit when the *hearing-impaired* listener and/or lipreader personally learns to recognize any sources of perceptual difficulty and then suggests the most appropriate and potentially effective methods of clarification* (see pp. 116-124).

In practice, we have applied an arbitrary rule to avoid excessive delays when a hearing-impaired listener cannot easily identify a message segment (Erber, 1982, 1985). If the listener still is unable to identify a particular word or phrase after three different remedial strategies have

---

* Following an encounter with unintelligible speech, a hearing-impaired communicator ideally should be able to correctly determine why it cannot be understood, and then work to resolve the problem. For example, the hearing-impaired person might suggest that the talker's speech intensity was too low, that the syllable rate was too rapid, or that the sentence was too long.

been applied, then that part of the message may simply be bypassed. The clinician notes the difficult item, however, for later discussion with the client. See Table 4-3 for examples of some words, phrases, and sentences that were very difficult for hearing-impaired communicators to identify.

Application of the Tracking Procedure usually takes the following form. The clinician might present the following sentence, part of a short story used as practice material during an auditory-visual Tracking session: "He carefully replaced the cup on the shelf." The hearing-impaired client must repeat what was just said. A typical response may include several misperceptions, for example, "He tearfully laced up his boots." Several words and a phrase have been perceived incorrectly. The clinician informs the client that the response was incorrect. The hearing-impaired person requests that the clinician repeat the entire sentence and speak more clearly. The clinician complies, and this time the client responds, "He tearfully laced up himself." The clinician indicates that only the first word has been identified correctly. The client requests that the sentence be presented another way. The clinician responds, "He put the cup on *the* shelf.", and the client repeats this simplified utterance correctly. The clinician indicates that she will add a word, and says: "He put the cup on the shelf..... *carefully*."

The client repeats this easily, and asks for presentation of the original sentence. The clinician follows this instruction, articulating precisely, applying exaggerated stress, and pausing between phrases: "He.....carefully *replaced*.....the cup on the shelf." The client thinks the clinician said, "He carefully.....something.....the cup on the shelf.", and asks that the first part of the sentence be repeated. The clinician agrees, but explains that first she will say it a simpler way, and then the original way: "He carefully put back the cup..... He carefully replaced the cup....." At this point, the hearing-impaired person exclaims: "I know! He carefully *replaced* the cup on the shelf." The clinician acknowledges this correct repetition, and then proceeds to the next sentence in the story.

In most cases, the Tracking Procedure is applied in this way, as one progresses through the chosen text. The clinician presents successive segments of verbal material, repeats utterances when requested by the

Table 4-3. Misperceptions are often revealed through use of Tracking (DeFilippo and Scott, 1978) or any other procedure that requires one to identify and repeat messages as they are received. Listed below are some auditory-visual errors exhibited by hearing-impaired adults during communication practice.

Stimulus	Response
lobster	monster
Lake Forest	leg force
hamburgers	handbags
marijuana	methadone
Eastlands	Woolworths
My ex-wife	Max's wife
translation	wrong station
lipreading	good breeding
radial fibers	Lady Godiva
car insurance	Koori shirts
six dinner rolls	sixteen rolls
Have you seen it?	Is he in it?
8 Deerfield Road	18 Field Road
realities of life	we are to survive
letting off steam	low self-esteem
He's over forty.	He's overly faulty.
bought it at cost	might have got lost
an 8-day clock	a night-and-day clock
my two housemates	my dear husband
do structured testing	destructive testing
It's got a walnut on top.	It's getting warm out.
Did it all go smoothly?	did an August medley
I've got to learn a little	You've got a wonderful
They're noxious vermin!	They're nice and furry!
Watch out for bike riders!	I have four typewriters.
Do you have a travel card?	Did you eat an avocado?
Do you have a lot to do?	Did you have a lobster too?
washing strewn all over	Russian streudel in the oven
What time does the film start?	What time does the sun set?
Are your classes helping you?	Are your glasses helping you?
Maybe it has sentimental value	maybe it is some Machiavelli
She has been very encouraging.	She says you're very intelligent.
Have you ever donated blood?	Have you ever gone out at night?
This town's so small, it's not even on the map!	This salad's so small, it's not even on the menu!

client, and applies clarification strategies, when necessary, to obtain per-fect/verbatim repetition from the hearing-impaired person.

A common approach is to present text for a fixed amount of time, such as 20 minutes*. Following that time period, the number of words spoken and also correctly repeated by the client is counted and noted. The clinician divides the total number of words spoken/repeated by the total time (in minutes) required for verbatim "tracking". This calculation yields a words-per-minute rate, which is a rough measure of communi-cation efficiency. The result permits the clinician to estimate how fluently the hearing-impaired client might communicate during an actual conversation.

Tracking is a very useful practice technique and is easy for both the client and clinician to learn. Both must remember at all times, however, that the goal is to complete the communication task as quickly as possible within each session. Progress from one session to the next often can be observed (Figure 4-1). A client's performance, however, can fluctuate considerably as a function of the content and style of the text, the speech clarity of the talker, and the methods used for applying various remedial strategies**.

USING CONTEXT TO ENHANCE INTELLIGIBILITY

Often, a hearing-impaired person will not be able to understand someone's spoken messages because the sensory information that is available simply is inadequate for intelligibility. That is, particular speech elements may be inaudible or unclear, and only fragments of the

---

* Some clinicians choose to complete a brief story or article of known length (number of words), and do *not* set a time limit. Instead, they simply note the time at which the practice activity begins and also when it ends, using the elapsed time to calculate the words-per-minute rate.

** Some clients/clinicians choose to apply a well-organized hierarchy of clarification strategies, always progressing through these in a fixed order when misperceptions occur. This approach, unfortunately, may contradict other problem-identification and problem-solving techniques (see pp. 116-124).

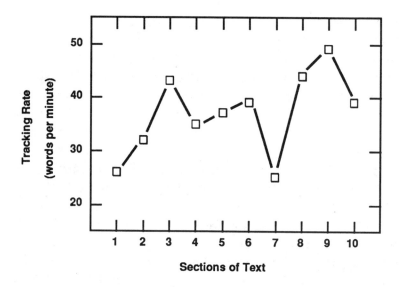

Figure 4-1. Results of ten consecutive 5-minute intervals ("sections") in which a clinician used the Tracking Procedure to provide practice in auditory-visual speech perception to a profoundly hearing-impaired 19 year-old male. The practice material consisted of paragraphs from a book on photography (after Owens and Telleen, 1981).

acoustic pattern are heard. In many instances, lipreading does not fully compensate, because the articulatory information that is needed is either ambiguous or is invisible. Under these difficult conditions, a given utterance may be perceived either as nonsense, as an incomplete message, or misperceived as a complete message other than that which the speaker intended.

When words or sentences are presented under the controlled conditions of an audiology clinic, they usually are uttered in an arbitrary sequence as the unrelated items of a test list. In contrast, most messages that are spoken in real life occur in a meaningful "context" - in a communication environment that surrounds the communicators, their interaction, the message, and its referents. In many cases, the surrounding environment may even have *stimulated* the speaker to produce the message. Some situations are so closely associated with the utterance of particular phrases, in fact, that one often can *anticipate* what the other person is going to say (e.g., flight attendant holding two steaming metal containers: "Tea or coffee?"; slinky blond woman with unlit cigarette: "Got a match?"). But the effects of context usually are both more subtle and pervasive than as shown in these cliches.

Contextual Benefits

Many contextual factors associated with discourse provide clues as to what people have just said, are now saying, or are about to say next. Sometimes these contextual effects are so strong that we can anticipate what people are going to say. We may even finish their sentences for them, before......*they* do.

A hearing-impaired communicator who is acutely aware of the conversational *context** is in a much better position to receive ambiguous messages with accuracy than is someone who relies exclusively on the somewhat distorted acoustic and optical speech information that he/she actually receives. That is, one who receives spoken sentences as if they were merely part of an unrelated sequence (as in a test list) is seriously disadvantaged. We have observed that a hearing-impaired person who makes use of all available contextual information usually will receive more of the message content correctly on the first presentation, will require fewer repetitions, will need to request fewer remedial clarifications from the speaker, and as a result will achieve greater conversational fluency.

Clinical experience suggests four main "contextual" aids to intelligibility: (1) environmental and situational factors; (2) word-order and word-associations within sentences; (3) inter-personal and inter-relational factors; and (4) sequential contingencies within conversations. In subsequent sections, we will discuss each factor, providing examples of related activities for communication therapy.

---

*   We may think of *context* as all the circumstances, events, or parts of discourse that precede, follow, or otherwise connect with a person's attempt to communicate.

Environmental and Situational Factors

A conversation always takes place *somewhere*, and usually between two or more people who are doing *something*. The environment in which the conversation takes place and the particular situation that prompted it often strongly influence what communicators say to one another. For example, if the conversation occurs in a restaurant, at least some of the conversation probably will be directed to the topics of food, drinks, waiters, or other restaurants. In addition, within the restaurant environment, even the immediate situation may affect the ongoing flow of the conversation: e.g., "I think the waiter is ignoring us." or "I'd like to tell the chef that this spaghetti marinara is delicious!".

Word Order and Word Associations (Syntax and Semantics)

We tend to use *words* to communicate, and we employ sequences of these words in agreed-upon linguistic patterns, such as phrases and sentences, to communicate efficiently. The grammar of our language specifies the order in which we must speak words within phrases or sentences to convey our intended meanings. These formalized rules of word order tend to produce some sentences that are highly redundant and thus predictable. For example, given the sentence fragment, "The carpenter hammered a _____.", we reasonably presume that this ordered sequence of words will end with a noun or perhaps an adjective-noun pair. Such rules of word *order* establish a particular degree of predictability and often allow a hearing-impaired person to fill in the gaps that result from misperceptions or nonperceptions.

Some words are so closely associated* with others that they frequently occur nearby, in the same sentence. Thus some connections between words are very strong, as the result of word pairings that describe people and what they often do (e.g., *children play*), between objects and their well-known attributes (e.g., *red rose*), and so forth. Also, words that fre-

---

* By "word association" we mean that perception of a word evokes a strong memory or image - and thus anticipation - of another, specific word. For example, which word do you think of - and thus expect to appear next - when I say: "mashed"?........*potatoes*, probably.

quently occur together in commonly used phrases or sequences are likely to be closely associated (e.g., *bread and butter; one , two , three*). As a result, if one is unable to perceive a spoken word clearly in a sentence, he/she may be able to guess what it might be just simply by reference to other associated words in that sentence. For example, in the sentence fragment concerning the *carpenter* referred to above, we might reasonably guess that the missing item in the sequence is *nail* , as this word often is uttered with the word *hammer(ed)*, and in addition, the word *nail* describes an object that carpenters frequently strike with hammers. So, sentences provide an organized framework for words, and a hearing-impaired person often can use this familiar linguistic context to re-construct ambiguously perceived messages (see Alyeshmerni and Taubr, 1975).

Inter-Personal Factors

The relationship between the communication partners also provides a degree of limiting context, that is, an inter-personal space in which only certain topics are likely to be discussed and certain levels of discourse reached (Watzlawick, Bavelas, and Jackson, 1967). For example, if the communicators have a range of shared experiences, shared background knowledge, similar feelings or common attitudes, then it is likely that they will interact within this familiar context. Knowing what the other person *thinks* or *feels* often is a clue to what he/she is likely to *say* in a particular situation.

But even if the communicators are unfamiliar with one another (i.e., they have just recently met), people quickly form impressions - based on a new awareness of the other's interests, personality, job, or role in a particular situation (e.g., someone collecting donations for earthquake victims). These presuppositions regarding the other person's role or personality, if correct, can guide one to accurately anticipate the content of spoken messages and also the style of social interaction to be followed (Clark and Clark, 1977). Moreover, the "feelings" the other communicator projects while speaking can provide a wide range of non-verbal prompts or clues to the nature or meaning of the utterance. Some examples are facial expression, eye contact, posture, and/or the gestures that accompany speech (Berger and Popelka, 1971; Argyle, 1975; Gerot, 1977).

Sequential Contingencies

In conversations, words, phrases, and sentences are exchanged, and each communicator stimulates and responds to the other's utterances. What one person says often can produce predictable responses in the other. The most common example is the typical result of saying, "Good morning!". Usually the other person will *greet* you in return. If you were to ask a specific question, the other person might *answer* in a somewhat predictable manner. A hearing-impaired individual often can use these sequential probabilities in conversation to anticipate the form of the other person's utterance - in response to whatever was previously spoken.

In addition to these short-range pragmatic ("stimulus-response") effects, there are powerful *cumulative* factors that also influence conversations. Over the course of several exchanges of phrases and sentences (turn-taking cycles), the communicators get to know one another and also develop conversational topics. Information, moods, attitudes, and opinions all accumulate as the result of the continuing interchange. As this growing context is created by the conversation itself - by the sequence of verbal exchanges - each communicator's expectations develop, based on his/her newly acquired knowledge of the other person's interests, feelings, and awareness. The more the communicators talk within a particular personal exchange, the more predictable the content of the conversation is likely to be, unless of course the topic is changed or a side issue is developed. A hearing-impaired person who is aware of this cumulative conversational context often can make informed guesses about ambiguously perceived utterances*.

---

* It is likely that ambiguous messages heard/seen toward the middle or end of a conversation - that is, after the communicators establish the topic, mood, direction, and intent - are much easier to interpret than those that appear earlier in the conversation, before its "context" has been developed. Accumulation of topic-related knowledge may influence reception of *narrative* as well, as for example in the Tracking Procedure (DeFilippo and Scott, 1978) (see pp. 95-99).

LANGUAGE-USE STRATEGIES

In most *linguistic* approaches to communication therapy, the intent is to show the hearing-impaired client how a person can use his/her latent knowledge of language to predict spoken responses, or to reconstruct or interpret ambiguous speech elements, fragments of sentences, or marginally intelligible spoken messages. The clinician can apply various forms of meta-communication* to direct the client's attention to word order in sentences, to word/phrase relations, and to conversational intents and sequences within contexts (see pp. 179-181). These may be described, respectively, as syntactic, semantic, and pragmatic activities.

Syntactic Approach

A language, such as English, incorporates a set of grammatical rules that specify the order in which one may utter words to communicate. For example, we may say, "The beans are purple.", "Are the beans purple?", or perhaps " ..... purple the beans are!". But we are not likely to say " ..... beans the purple are .....", if we desire to interact easily with others who speak our language.

Often, a hearing-impaired person will not perceive every word in a sentence. Sometimes, he/she is able to quickly fill the perceptual gaps by making informed "guesses", basing these guesses on what people are known to say in particular situations. Some hearing-impaired people, however, have difficulty making conscious hypotheses regarding the composition of misperceived sentence fragments. They do not know, for example, that they have misperceived a noun in the sentence or perhaps a passive verb construction, and so they are unable to correct the perceptual error by "filling in" with appropriate word forms.

In such cases, remedial activities may include giving the hearing-impaired client specific practice in reconstructing incompletely received spoken messages (Hull, 1976). Here, we help the client become more aware of his/her accumulated knowledge of common word order, morphology, and ideomatic structures, and we also show the client that he/she can effectively use this underlying linguistic framework to help

---

* *Meta-communication* is the ability to think about communication, and to talk about it.

Table 4-4. Examples of some sentence frames used in syntactic practice.

a. Nonsense	b. Real words
Why do stogs _____?	_____ is not here.
_____ rizzled in the korm.	How many _____?
Flim the _____ in the drox!	The _____ was _____ by the _____.
_____ will grosh.	_____ is _____.
The flast _____ and _____.	Where is _____?
_____ a strek in the glinz.	Does it _____?
Morgats zilp _____.	After _____, we _____.
_____ the murl.	I _____, but you _____.
Firmaks _____ under the lep.	_____ are not _____ in the _____.
The lan is _____.	I'm so _____ that _____.

clarify incompletely perceived utterances.

In practice sessions, the major portion of each sentence is presented audio-visually, but key items are presented as gaps in the message: spoken as "......buzz-buzz......", without voice, and/or behind an opaque barrier such as a card or the clinician's hand (Erber, 1982). Alternatively, the sentences may be presented directly in printed form, with their gaps shown as blank spaces (Hull, 1976) (Table 4-4a,b). To minimize semantic content (meaning and associative cues), numerous nonsense forms may be substituted for real words (see Berko, 1958; Woodward, 1964). Item difficulty can be varied in this way, or by constructing sentence frames that differ in syntactic complexity.

The client is asked to apply his/her knowledge of word and phrase order and to "guess" what might have been spoken during the interval (which is meant to represent perceptual ambiguity). For example, sentence frames such as "_____ _____ is not here!" or "_____ _____ blaned flinkingly." should elicit noun phrases in response. Thus, acceptable responses might be *"Michael's bicycle* is not here!", *"Her horse* blaned flinkingly.", or perhaps *"The snurg* blaned flinkingly.". In this exercise, the specific words that are provided by the hearing-impaired person to fill the gaps are not important.

Semantic Approach

The formal organization of language and the rules that govern word *order* are not the only linguistic clues that allow one to re-construct misperceived sentence fragments. The words that are contained in sentences also tend to be meaningfully (semantically) *related* to one another. For example, most people recognize a close association between the two words in the sentence, "Birds fly." as this pair elicits a familiar image, whereas most people see little relation between the two words in the sentence, "Birds meditate.", as together, these words describe an improbable event. It seems that a close semantic relationship between words results partly from: (a) frequent pairing of the words themselves in verbal communication (e.g., "Once upon a time" or "babbling brook"); and (b) frequent pairing of their referents in real life, i.e., the actual events or physical states that the word-symbols represent (e.g., "bouncing ball", or "green leaves").

Some hearing-impaired clients do not realize that they may be able to accurately fill perceptual gaps or "guess" the identity of ambiguously perceived fragments of spoken messages by considering the semantic relationships of these units to other, adjacent words or phrases in the utterance (e.g., as in the sentence, "The young girl combed her long, blond *eh*."). We attempt to show each client that unclear words within sentences (or even within lists) often can be identified on the basis of their meaningful associations with neighbouring words and phrases which were confidently perceived (either before or after) in the sequence.

For example, the clinician may point out the close associations between the (referents of) common words in particular classes (e.g., animals, tools, flowers, colours, clothing), between words within common phrases, between a noun phrase and a verb phrase within the same sentence, or even between the contents of successive sentences that form part of a narrative. Some examples are given in Table 4-5a,b,c,d.

In practice sessions, the hearing-impaired client is asked to fill gaps (representing misperceptions) in spoken or printed word sequences, phrases, or sentences (Table 4-6a,b) (Jeffers and Barley, 1971; Hull, 1976; Chermak, 1981). This task often can be done easily, on the basis of known relationships between items in particular categories (e.g., car, bus, train,

Table 4-5. Examples of semantic relationships.

a. Associated words (Entwisle, 1966)

short: long, tall, fat
sheep: wool, lamb, animal
loud: soft, noise, quiet
dark: light, night, black
chair: table, sit, seat

thirsty: water, drink, dry
hand: foot, arm, finger
smooth: rough, soft, hard
bitter: sweet, sour, taste
needle: thread, pin, sharp

b. Common phrases containing associated words (Alyeshmerni and Taubr, 1975)

a cup of coffee
rich or poor
bread and butter
slow as a turtle
law and order

bacon and eggs
eat like a pig
a bowl of cereal
sticks and stones
stubborn as a mule

c. Redundant/predictive sentences (Kalikow, Stevens, and Elliott, 1977)

Football is a dangerous sport.
On the beach we play in the sand.
A bear has a thick coat of fur.
The little girl cuddled her doll.
We heard the ticking of the clock.

Stir your coffee with a spoon.
We saw a flock of wild geese.
This key won't fit in the lock.
A rose bush has prickly thorns.
The dealer shuffled the cards.

d. Successive sentences: narrative (Jeffers and Barley, 1971; see Prince, 1982)

One sunny morning, Jimmy woke up early.
He jumped out of bed.
He put on his cowboy hat and galloped into the kitchen.
Mother was still in her curlers.
She gave him breakfast.
He had orange juice, cereal, and milk.
Jimmy went outside.
He met another cowboy.
The two cowboys rode the range together.

_____), between people and what they frequently say or do (e.g., "Plumbers fix clogged _____."), between referents and their well-known attributes (e.g., "The soft, furry _____ meowed hungrily."), and so forth. The client is shown how easily one may fill gaps in related sequences like these. Alternatively, misperceptions may be shown, not as blank spaces, but as likely error responses instead, such as "My friend bought a pair of red leather *candles* to match her new dress.".

We have noted that phrases or sentences vary considerably in their internal redundancy. Some do not provide as much useful predictive/associative context as others (Kalikow, Stevens, and Elliott, 1977) (see Table 4-5c). For example, in the sentence, "Would you please find *operculum* for me in the dictionary?", the numerous words surrounding *operculum* tell us that it also is a *word*, but they give us no clue as to its identity.

Moreover, in some real-life situations, the hearing-impaired person may misperceive the *surrounding* sentence fragments as well as misperceive the "key" words. Consequently, he/she may construct an incorrect sentence frame and thus generate an incorrect associative context. The semantic misdirection that results may lead to gross errors in identification of the target words, in spite of contradictory (potentially "correct") sensory input that these target words provide. For example, one hearing-impaired person misperceived the sentence, "I parked the van at my house." as, "I picked up a cat and mouse." According to the client, this occurred because she identified the words *my house* confidently as *mouse*, the words *I parked* as *I picked*, and simply forced the remainder of the sentence into this self-created framework.

Pragmatic Approach

In general, conversations consist of the purposeful interchange of ideas by two (or more) people. To avoid confusion, the participants usually agree on an orderly method of talking. This learned verbal system of communication is governed by a variety of generally accepted "rules", such as: communicators should be truthful, informative, topic-relevant, and unambiguous (Grice, 1975); each person should have a

Table 4-6. Examples of list/sentence frames used in semantic practice.

a. **Lists: client supplies missing word**

giraffe, elephant, _____, lion, chimpanzee, zebra
shirt, coat, boots, belt, hat, _____, scarf, gloves
steak, _____, bacon, fish, hamburger, chicken
apricot, pineapple, _____, watermelon, orange
chair, lamp, bed, bookcase, table, couch, _____
wrench, screwdriver, pliers, _____, saw, drill
chocolate cake, plum pudding, ice cream, _____

b. **Sentence frames; client supplies missing word**

Highly predictable:
He was so angry, he slammed the _____.
My car has another flat _____.
Please wipe your _____ on the mat.
Don't forget to water the _____!
The little girl clapped her _____.
Dig the _____ over here, by this bush.
He baked a _____ for her birthday.
Would you like another cup of _____?

Moderately predictable:
My dog refuses to eat _____.
We've just moved to South _____.
She and her husband have _____ children.
The _____ flew away when we got close.
He gave the _____ bicycle to the boy.
This radio has a broken _____.
We fed some bread to the _____.
We saw _____ in the barn.

Not very predictable:
We often talked about the _____.
After dinner, she showed me the _____.
I just bought a _____.
He didn't know about the _____.
Please don't ask me about the _____!
I've never heard of a _____.
Do you have a _____?
We couldn't remember the name of the _____.

regular opportunity to talk; only one person should talk at any given time; procedures should indicate when it is the other person's turn to talk (Clark and Clark, 1977). Turns are taken and relinquished according to social conventions as well, such as: eye contact, facial expression, gesture, posture, voice level and pitch, pause, prompting, and so forth (Duncan, 1972; Sacks, Schegloff, and Jefferson, 1974; Weiner and Goodenough, 1977).

Contingent pairs

There are many other aspects to the turn-taking sequence in conversation, however - ones pertaining to the requirements of the specific verbal interchange. For example, what one communicator says can directly influence what the other communicator is likely to say in response.

This psycholinguistic concept suggests that the general form of a communication partner's verbal *response* often can be predicted, given that the first speaker (e.g., a hearing-impaired person) has previously produced a particular form of verbal stimulus (Clark and Clark, 1977). This stimulus-response effect is very strong. For example, when one person greets another, the second usually responds with a similar *greeting* ("Hi, Helen!"..."Oh, hello Norm; it's good to see you!"). A question usually elicits an *answer* ("Where did you get your old cast-iron stove?"..."At a junk shop in Richmond."). A compliment tends to elicit an *acknowledgement* ("Your New Year's Eve party was really fun!" .... "Thanks! We spent weeks planning it.") (Table 4-7).

Most experienced communicators intuitively recognize the close association between what they say and the way that others respond to their utterances. Hearing-impaired people can use their awareness of these sequential tendencies to predict what other people might say to them at particular times during a conversation.

One can provide hearing-impaired clients with directed practice in anticipating the form and content of utterances that others are likely to produce in response to specific verbal stimuli. For example, the clinician may construct a list of typical conversational topics and also a list of

Table 4-7. Some examples of "contingent pairs". What one person says (stimulus) can limit what the other person is likely to say (response).

Greeting: "Hello, Cam!"
Greeting: "Hiya, Jan!"

Question: "Say, how're you getting to work tomorrow?"
Answer: "Oh, I'll probably drive in, as usual."

Request: "Well, could you pick me up?"
Grant/Refusal: "Yeah ..... It's on my way!"

Offer: "Should I wait at the corner?"
Acceptance/rejection: "Nah! I'll stop by your house - at about 8:15."

Compliment: "Your new Delta XZ looks great!"
Acceptance/rejection: "Thanks! I washed and polished it on Sunday."

Assertion: "Oh, I can't stand the sound of squealing tires!"
Acknowledgement: "Yeah, I know ....."
or
Agreement/Disagreement: "Well, it doesn't bother *me*!"
or
Elaboration: "I'll lose my job if I'm late for work again!"
or
Question: "Are you criticizing my driving?"

---

related statements or questions (Table 4-8). The hearing-impaired client is asked to present an item from the prepared list (e.g., FILMS: "Did you watch *Casablanca* on TV last night?"). Then, he/she must predict what a frequent communication partner is likely to say in response (e.g., "Yeah; that was the 18th time!" or "No, I missed it."). This practice procedure provides the client with numerous realistic, conversation-like experiences. In a very short time during the session, the client is able to participate in a wide range of verbal stimulus-response exchanges, noting numerous contingent-pair associations.

Table 4-8. Examples of conversational topics/contexts and related "contingent" stimulus-response pairs used in communication practice.

Topic/utterance	Expected response
WEATHER: "It looks pretty cloudy outside!"	("_____")
ILLNESSES: "Everyone in our family has a bad cold!"	("_____")
FRIEND'S BIRTHDAY: "How many people will be at your party?"	("_____")
TALKING TO A NEIGHBOUR: "Could I borrow your lawnmower?"	("_____")
AT A SANDWICH BAR: "You make great sandwiches!"	("_____")
AT WORK ON MONDAY MORNING: "I'm so tired!"	("_____")
BREAKFAST TABLE: "Is the coffee ready yet?"	("_____")
GREETING A FRIEND: "Hi, Jennie!"	("_____")
WATCHING TELEVISION: "This program is really boring!"	("_____")
AT A HARDWARE STORE: "I want to buy an extension cord."	("_____")

Contingent pairs, however, differ greatly in their associative strength, and thus one's ability to predict the other communicator's response may fluctuate. One contingent pair sequence whose outcome is much less secure than the others is that which begins with an *assertion* (a descriptive statement, an opinion, or an expression of one's feelings) - which may be followed by an acknowledgement, agreement/disagreement, an elaboration, or even a question. For example, the statement, "I'm not feeling very well this morning." may elicit the sympathetic response, "Oh, I'm sorry to hear that, dear. Maybe you should stay in bed today." It has been suggested that making assertions demonstrates trust in one's communication partner - expecially confidence in his/her personality and interactive style (Luterman, 1984). That is, one tends to make assertions only after becoming familiar with the other communicator.

When a speaker makes an outright assertion, he/she is expressing a personal observation, attitude, feeling, or opinion, and is essentially inviting the other communicator to do the same in response. That is, the speaker is taking a *chance* (playing "conversational roulette"?) with the other communicator. And so, it also is possible that the statement, "I'm not feeling very well this morning." will elicit the unsympathetic response, "You irresponsible moron!" I told you not to drink so much last night at the party!".

Situational context

Daily situations, or the environmental contexts in which conversations occur, also can help one to anticipate the substance of verbal messages. We often expect people to express themselves in ways that are appropriate to the roles they play. For example, if a boy scout arrives at your door with a large box of specially wrapped chocolate bars, he can be expected to say something like: "Hello. We're selling chocolate to raise money...". With a little practice, a hearing-impaired person can learn to employ similar contextual prompts to predict the content of numerous utterances. Several clinical evaluation and practice procedures have been based on this principle (see Morkovin, 1947; Garstecki and O'Neill, 1980; Jeffers and Barley, 1971; Chermak, 1981) (Table 4-9).

We must realize, however, that environmental contexts vary greatly in the extent to which they circumscribe verbal communication (see Table 4-10). That is, some conversational situations tend to greatly limit what people are likely to say (e.g., the scene of a serious auto accident),

Table 4-9. Context has a strong effect on the type of message that is spoken.

A. Utterances overheard in various *situations*

SHOPPING FOR NECKLACE: "The jewellery in this shop is so expensive!"

WAITING FOR BUS: "I'm going to be late for work again!"

EATING LUNCH IN RESTAURANT: "Everything on this menu is in *French!*"

CHECKING OUT IN SUPERMARKET: "I hope I have enough money to pay for all this."

WAITING FOR DOCTOR: "I wish all these waiting-room magazines weren't so *old.*"

AT A PLAY: "Did you read the review in yesterday's newspaper?"

B. Messages spoken by various *people*

MOTHER: "Go and ask your father!"

SISTER: "Have you borrowed my new red belt?"

OLD FRIEND: "Are you still married to *Steve*?"

NEW FRIEND: "Are you a Scorpio?"

COLLEGE INSTRUCTOR: "I'd like that assignment in two weeks."

DOCTOR: "How long have you had this pain?"

POLICEMAN: "You have the right to remain silent....."

STRANGER IN BUILDING: "Where is the director's office please?"

Table 4-10. The predictability of language behaviour varies, depending on the particular situation and the conversational context.

A. Non-limiting context, unpredictable content -

Stranger, sitting beside you on a bus: "Excuse me. Do you have a pencil that I could borrow?"

B. Moderately limiting context, moderately predictable content -

Husband, looking up from newspaper: "Did you know that the price of milk is going up three cents on Monday?"

C. Limiting context, limited content -

Waitress in restaurant, after you have studied the menu for a few minutes: "Would you like to order now?"

---

while others are relatively non-restricting and lead to open-ended, multiple-topic conversations (e.g., a long, comfortable bus ride).

Problems

Effective use of sensory input, awareness of linguistic factors and conversational contingencies, appropriate daily experiences, and clinical guidance all will lead the client to better management of communication. Regardless, most hearing-impaired people will continue to experience occasional gaps in conversational fluency that result from misperception, misanticipation, and/or misdirection. These brief periods of conversational confusion probably are inevitable. Even normal-hearing people experience occasional communication difficulties - as the result of background noise, environmental distractions, and encounters with unfamiliar topics - but of course less frequently than do hearing-impaired people. Because hearing-impaired communicators can expect momentary disruptions in their conversations, they can benefit from *preparing* for such occurrences. That is, they can become familiar with the most likely sources of personal difficulty, and they can acquire a set of well-practised remedial strategies to apply should it be necessary to "repair" a conversation (see Lubinski, Duchan, and Weitzner-Lin, 1980).

Problem-solving

A *problem-solving* approach can be applied to the resolution of most common communication breakdowns (Erber and Greer, 1973; DeFilippo and Scott, 1978; Owens and Telleen, 1981). There are several identifiable steps in one's personal remediation process (see Demorest, 1986):

    (1) recognize that a conversational dysfluency has occurred;

    (2) identify the source/cause of the difficulty;

    (3) select, request, and/or apply an appropriate corrective strategy to overcome the problem;

    (4) judge the effectiveness of the strategy (e.g., increased clarity of the speaker's next attempt to communicate);

    (5) confirm that the correct message was received (e.g., "Did you say...?);

    (6) if the message was received correctly, continue the conversation;

    (7) if the last strategy that was applied was ineffective, and it failed to resolve the difficulty, consider why it failed (e.g., source of original difficulty misjudged; or strategy not applied correctly);

    (8) request/apply the original strategy more appropriately, or...

    (9) select an alternative strategy to suggest or attempt next;

    (10) (then return to step number 4).

We will discuss several of the steps in this remediation process. There are numerous reasons that conversations break down, that is, become misdirected and thus confusing for the communicators. Some of these causes are listed in Table 4-11. Either communicator, the topic or content, and/or the surrounding environment may be the disruptive influence.

Awareness of all these possible sources of difficulty is just an initial step, however. It is much more important to be able to correctly identify the cause of a *specific* communication breakdown that is encountered *as the conversation is in progress*. That is, the hearing-impaired person must

Table 4-11. Some potential sources of difficulty in face-to-face conversation.

Hearing-impaired person:

A. Inability to detect, discriminate, or identify units of speech
B. Poor understanding of one's own perceptual limitations
C. Poor meta-communication skills
D. Poor planning for the conversation
E. Incorrect setting or malfunction of hearing aids
F. Personal discomfort, resulting from fatigue or illness
G. Inattention

Message structure or content:

A. Unfamiliar topic; abrupt shifts in topic
B. Uncommon words, technical terms, jargon
C. Colloquial expressions
D. Unusually long sentences
E. Complex syntax (e.g., passive verb, embedded clause)
F. Several sentences presented in succession (narrative)

Communication partner's speech:

A. Syllable rate too rapid
B. Voice level too low, fluctuates, decreases
C. Voice pitch too high, fluctuates, increases
D. Careless articulation
E. Foreign or regional accent: unusual prosody/intonation/stress
F. Head moves during speech production
G. Mouth/face obscured by hand, hair, object
H. Lack of awareness/cooperation re clarification strategies

Communication environment:

A. Great distance between communicators
B. High noise level
C. Excessive reverberation
D. Low illumination level
E. Glare from reflecting objects
G. Visible distractions

be able to analytically examine the ongoing conversation and its surrounding environment (or his/her recent memory of it) for potential
sources of personal confusion. This cognitive process can be difficult for
some hearing-impaired people to manage (Cohen, 1987).

Once the hearing-impaired person thinks he/she has identified the
source of the communication problem, he/she then requests a change in
the content of the utterance or a change in its manner of presentation.
Some well-known message-clarification strategies are listed in Table 4-
12 (see Erber and Greer, 1973). These are *remedial* strategies; numerous
preparatory strategies also exist, such as: be certain that there are fresh
batteries in the hearing aids; make sure that the room is quiet; arrange the
furniture or light sources for optimal illumination of the speaker's face;
and so forth (Kaplan, 1982; McCall, 1984).

When conversational fluency is disrupted, the hearing-impaired
person may realize that he/she has misunderstood, but may not be sure
why. Consequently he/she may request, in a relatively nonspecific
manner, that the speaker simply *repeat* the message (see Table 4-13). If the
communication partner repeats *exactly*, however, that person may inad-
vertently re-create the same disruptive effect as before. Of course, it is
much more productive for the hearing-impaired communicator to examine the ongoing conversation carefully so that the reason for the dysfluency can be deduced. Because there are so many possible and likely
causes of communication breakdown, however, the hearing-impaired
communicator may fail to correctly identify the source of confusion in
his/her first attempt, or may even be reluctant to admit any personal
confusion at all (see Table 4-14).

Recognizing the source of difficulty

An important part of the problem-solving process involves correctly
identifying the source of conversational dysfluency. The hearing-impaired person may not be adequately prepared, or the hearing aids may
not be functioning. The client's linguistic or meta-linguistic abilities may
be undeveloped. Often, the problem can be directly attributed to
distractions from (or masking by) the environment. At other times, the
communication partner may have spoken unclearly or may have pre-

Table 4-12. Some message-clarification strategies that can be applied if communication difficulty occurs.

The speaker may:

1. Present message again	a. Repeat entire utterance
	b. Repeat first/last part
2. Speak more clearly	a. Reduce syllable rate
	b. Increase overall loudness
	c. Reduce voice pitch
	d. Emphasize key words
	e. Pause before/after key words
	f. Increase articulatory precision
3. Substitute word/phrase	a. Synonym
	b. Equivalent phrase
4. Prompt with related words	a. Noun-noun sequence
	b. Noun-verb sequence
	c. Adjective-noun sequence
5. Modify message	a. Use more common words/phrases
	b. Simplify word order
	c. Add/delete a word/phrase
	d. Increase message redundancy
6. Give more information	a. Identify most important concept
	b. Describe prior/later events
	c. Present associated words/phrases
7. Provide non-verbal cues	a. Employ natural gestures
	b. Use meaningful facial expressions
	c. Employ appropriate posture
8. Present referent	a. Point to related object
	b. Refer to drawing/photo/map
9. Do something different	a. Talk about something else
	b. Try again later

Table 4-13. Some examples of (a) non-specific and (b) specific requests for clarification, in response to various communication difficulties.

a. **Non-specific requests (A.T.)**

Difficulty	Clarification request
Reduced volume:	"What's that?"
Increased rate:	"I didn't quite get that ....."
Long/complex:	"Sorry. What was that?"
Hand over mouth:	"I lost a bit of that ....."
Turned away:	"I didn't hear you."
Combinations of above:	"mmm..... What's that again?"

b. **Specific requests (J.P.)**

Difficulty	Clarification request
Reduced volume:	"Please speak up - your voice is too low."
Increased rate:	"Could you please slow down a little?"
Long/complex:	"I didn't hear the last part of that ....."
Hand over mouth:	"Could you put your hand down please?"
Turned away:	"Please face toward me when you speak."
Combinations of above:	"Did you say you lived in ... *Bairnsdale*?"

sented an unusually complex message. It is common for several of these disruptive sources to be present concurrently.

We have found that our hearing-impaired clients can benefit from specific practice which requires them to recognize and respond to particular sources of conversational disruption. We use a large set of stimulus sentences (e.g., see Table 3-6), which we select and present either live or via videotape. The sentences are spoken normally/clearly and also with many different sources of communication difficulty super-imposed - such as reduced voice level, careless articulation, or obscured

Table 4-14. Some reasons that a hearing-impaired person may not request clarification from a communication partner.

The hearing-impaired person:

is not aware of the effects of his/her own hearing loss on fluency and naturalness in conversation

does not recognize when communication difficulties have occurrred

lacks well-developed meta-communcation abilities and thus cannot think about or discuss conversational problems in a logical and coherent manner

feels that communication partners are responsible for resolving any communication difficulties that occur

can describe his/her communication problem, but seems unwilling or unable to do anything about it - feels incapable, helpless, or depressed

knows that a general communication problem exists, but is unable to correctly identify specific sources of difficulty

lacks confidence, perhaps as the result of previous errors in identifying sources of conversational difficulty

generally lacks assertiveness, and feels uncomfortable about asking another person to help or to change his/her behavior

feels that particular situations and contexts are not appropriate for the application of clarification procedures which might disrupt conversations

believes that communication partners will respond negatively to any requests for clarification (e.g., with exaggerated mouth movements, shouting, lack of empathy or cooperation, patronizing attitude, ridicule, expression of disgust)

feels that most members of society do not accept: (a) telling others about one's problems, confusions, and/or insecurities; (2) describing the faults of others, particularly communication partners; (c) discussing "conversation" in the middle of a conversation (i.e., meta-communication)

is unable to generalize "known" principles of clarification to specific conversational situations

---

Table 4-15. To promote the client's use of clarification requests, the clinician may communicate in the following ways.

Speak in ways that make speech reception difficult, such as:

> speak with high voice pitch
> speak rapidly
> speak softly
> lower voice level at the ends of sentences
> reduce acoustic clarity of articulations
> reduce visible clarity of articulations
> obscure the mouth
> turn the head while speaking
> tilt the head while speaking
> use distracting gestures

Present messages and employ syntactic constructions that are difficult to understand, such as:

> rare words, colloquialisms, or jargon
> inverted sentences
> yes/no questions
> long, complicated sentences
> inanimate subjects
> embedded clauses
> passive verb forms

visibility (see Table 4-15). After attending to each sentence, the hearing-impaired client is required to: (1) identify (repeat) the message, if possible; and (2) identify any source(s) of difficulty - even if the sentence was understood.

We also provide this type of problem-identification practice during most simulated conversations (e.g., TOPICON or QUEST?AR sessions: see pp. 75-85; 124-129). Realistic practice of this sort helps the hearing-

Table 4-16. Recognizing sources of potential communication difficulty. At different times during a brief simulated conversation (TOPICON, pp. 75-85), a clinician intentionally modified her speech and language to create receptive difficulty. The various types of disruption were randomly superimposed on spoken sentences, five times each. A hearing-impaired adult (R.M., male, 61 years) was asked to identify each type of disruption whenever it occurred. The results, summarized below, indicate that some sources of potential difficulty were harder to identify than others.

		Potential source of difficulty				
		Obscured mouth	Low voice level	Rapid speech	Careless artic.	Complex sentence
Identified?	Yes:	5	5	3	3	1
	No:	0	0	2	2	4

impaired person develop his/her meta-communication skills while participating in an interactive activity. Live presentations allow a natural conversational interchange to occur between the client and the clinician, and the client gains valuable experience from actually requesting, and receiving, appropriate clarification from a speaker (Table 4-16).

QUEST?AR (Questions for Aural Rehabilitation)

QUEST?AR* (Erber, 1985) is a conversation-based communication therapy procedure that provides interactive practice with numerous common question-answer sequences (see Binnie, 1976). During this

---

* QUEST?AR is published and distributed by HELOGRAPHICS, 12 Cook Street, Abbotsford, Victoria 3067, Australia.

practice activity, clients learn to anticipate and accurately receive spoken responses to familiar question forms.

QUEST?AR originally was created to provide communication practice to hearing-impaired adults who lack confidence in their ability to obtain spoken information, who don't readily ask questions during conversations (i.e., who ordinarily *dominate* conversations by presenting information), or who require practice participating in conversational formats in which question-answer sequences are prominent (Erber, 1985). QUEST?AR provides a framework for guided/simulated *conversations*. In the clinic, QUEST?AR can be used to provide practice in listening, lipreading, or in bisensory reception of ongoing speech - whichever type of communication experience the hearing-impaired client requires.

QUEST?AR materials include a printed list of 48 possible topics for conversation, and a booklet that contains a sequence of 30 inter-related questions (Table 4-17). Each conversational topic is a *place* that the clinician (presumably) has recently visited (e.g., Paris, Kakadu National Park, the Botanical Gardens, Katie's House of Fashion, a friend's house, a hardware store). The prepared sequence of questions provides a means for the hearing-impaired client to systematically find out about the clinician's visit (e.g., "What was the most interesting thing you saw?").

To apply QUEST?AR in the clinic, the hearing-impaired person first is given the printed booklet containing a set of simple instructions as well as the 30 questions (see Figure 4-2). He/she then begins the guided conversation by asking the topic-eliciting question, "Where did you go?". If the clinician cannot think of an interesting topic, he/she selects one by referring to the list of "Places" (perhaps before the session). To establish this topic unambiguously, the clinician answers the client's initial question by displaying the printed name of the place (e.g., Nairobi, Newmarket Shopping Centre, the beach, my back yard) - before the actual conversation begins. If necessary, a photo or drawing also may be presented to orient the client. Regardless of how the clinician *begins* the conversation, the client's subsequent task is to ask each prepared question in sequence, obtaining the *answer* to each one before proceeding to the next.

Table 4-17. Topics and questions from QUEST?AR * (Erber,1985)

Where did you go?	museum, restaurant, post office, shopping, camping, doctor, zoo, beach, airport, swimming, mountains, picnic, music lesson, Mars, supermarket, and so forth

Questions:
 1. Why did you go there?
 2. When did you go?
 3. How many people went with you?
 4. Who were they? (names)
 5. What did you take with you?
 6. Where is (the place where you went)?
 7. How did you get there?
 8. What did you see on the way?
 9. What time did you get there?
10. What did you do first?
11. What did you see?
12. How many? What colour? etc.
13. What happened at (the place where you went)?
14. What else did you do?
15. What were other people doing at (the place where you went)?
16. What was the most interesting thing that you saw?
17. What was the most interesting thing that you did?
18. What did you buy?
19. What kind? What flavour? What colour? etc.
20. How much did it cost?
21. Did anything unusual happen? What?
22. How long did you stay?
23. What did you do just before you came home?
24. When did you leave?
25. How did you get home?
26. What happened on the way home?
27. What time did you get home?
28. How did you feel then?
29. When are you going back?
30. Do you think that I should go sometime? Why?

* **QUEST**ions for Aural Rehabilitation

Figure 4-2. A page from the QUEST?AR booklet.

If the client cannot immediately understand any of the clinician's spoken auditory, visual, or auditory-visual responses, he/she should request appropriate repetition or clarification (see pp. 119-121). Clarification strategies often can be applied quite naturally during a QUEST?AR session, if both participants treat this clinical activity as if it were a real conversation rather than a simulation exercise in the form of a "half-script" (Erber, 1985). For example:

> Clinician: ...
> Client: "What did you buy?"
> Clinician: "A new skirt."
> Client: "Did you say a *shirt*?"
> Clinician: "No. I said a new *skirt*."
> Client: "Please say that a bit more slowly."
> Clinician: "A ..... *new* ..... *skirt*."

> Client: "I still don't understand. Could you please give me a little
> more information?"
> Clinician: "I bought a 'wrap-around' skirt."
> Client: "Oh! A new *skirt!*"
> Clinician: "Yes! That's right!"
> Client: "Good. Yeah, you mentioned that they were having a sale
> at Brubaker's! Well, how much did it cost?"
> Clinician: ...

The clinician should note the beginning and ending times of each QUEST?AR session, to roughly estimate the client's conversational efficiency, expressed in terms of the number of minutes required to obtain correct (intelligible) answers to all thirty questions. Of course, this "score" will improve not only with the client's increasing experience and competence with question-answer sequences, but it may fluctuate as well on the basis of general *topic* ("place") familiarity, and also the nature of the specific *answers* that one provides (e.g., common vs unfamiliar words; one-word vs whole-sentence responses). Therefore, the "score" (time required for completion) should be considered only as a general estimate of the client's conversational ability.

It is very important to discuss the entire interactive process with the client following each QUEST?AR practice session, examining particular conversational sequences that were easy or difficult and also strategies that were effective or inappropriate. Review of audio (or video) tapes, that have been recorded during the sessions, also can be very informative regarding the detailed communicative behaviours of each participant.

Many clients have commented that this interactive procedure, in which *they* ask the questions rather than an examiner or therapist, gives them confidence as communicators (i.e., it is easier), because they often can anticipate the form or content of many of the answers. That is, the spoken message that they receive in response is not unlimited, but instead is greatly restricted both by the chosen context (e.g., a recent visit to the science museum) and by the nature of each question (e.g., "What time did you get home?"). For example, in response to the client's question, "How did you get there?", the clinician is likely to say one of the following: "I walked; I rode my bicycle; I drove my car; I took the train".

Some clients get so interested in these simulated "conversations" that they insert related questions that do not even appear in the prescribed sequence of the QUEST?AR booklet (e.g., "How did the boy get his sock out of the tree?" or "Did you remember to turn off the radio?"). They ask these additional questions because they are actually interested in the content of the conversation and want to know more about the outcome of your story. Although this question-insertion process will invalidate "scoring" (timing) somewhat, one should not discourage a client from asking additional *related* questions of this sort. It provides desired practice, and promotes purposeful involvement in *real* interactive conversations.

ASQUE>>> (Answers/Statements/Questions)*

Under ideal conditions, hearing-impaired people can overcome most of their perceptual limitations by carefully monitoring and guiding the content of their conversations. That is, they usually can attain conversational fluency by interacting in such a way that the form of received responses is somewhat restricted and predictable. Achieving understanding by this process, however, requires that both communicators exhibit a considerable degree of linguistic awareness, cooperation, and skill in meta-communication.

The QUEST?AR procedure (see pp. 124-129) was designed to give hearing-impaired clients experience in directing conversations. During QUEST?AR practice sessions, in which 30 topic-related questions are presented, most clients notice that the clinician's *answers* vary in intelligibility. Sometimes, they recognize that the other communicator's response at each point in the sequence varies in predictability as a function of what *they* have just uttered as a stimulus. That is, some question (and statement) forms are found to be much more directive and

---

* ASQUE>>> materials are published and distributed by HELOGRAPHICS, 12 Cook Street, Abbotsford, Victoria 3067, Australia

limiting than others, greatly restricting the range of possible responses that the communication partner can present. If the hearing-impaired person is able to *consciously* narrow this range of possible responses, he/she can more easily predict what the communication partner is likely to say, and thus can more accurately synthesize and interpret those items that are perceptually unclear. Practice with selected Contingent Pair exercises also can demonstrate this effect (see pp. 111-114).

Our clinical experiences have suggested that the *type* of initiating question or statement that one produces has a very strong effect on the intelligibility of a speaker's *response*. This effect on understanding is especially apparent if the listener has a serious hearing loss and thus tends to receive the speaker's messages as fragmented or greatly distorted. A person's ability to identify a sentence appears to be directly related to the number of alternative messages that his/her communication partner is likely to present (Miller, Heise, and Lichten, 1951; Sumby and Pollack, 1954). The intelligibility of a spoken sentence also seems to be related to how closely (semantically) it maintains the topic of the stimulus sentence that preceded it. For example, the somewhat predictable response that follows a limited-choice question tends to be much easier for a hearing-impaired client to recognize than is the much less restricted response to a statement/assertion* (see Figure 4-3).

We frequently wish to clearly demonstrate to our clients the conversation-controlling power of their utterances. That is, we often want to show them how different types of contingent-pair initiators affect the potential intelligibility of subsequent responses. The purposes are: to demonstrate the differences between *limiting* and *non-limiting* stimuli; and to indicate how their initiating utterances influence the range of conversational conditions in which they can/cannot communicate easily.

---

* The stimulus category called "statements" (or assertions) contains: requests and commands (typical response: acceptance/refusal); opinions (typical response: agree/disagree); wants and needs (typical response: offer/rejection); descriptions (responses are very difficult to predict).

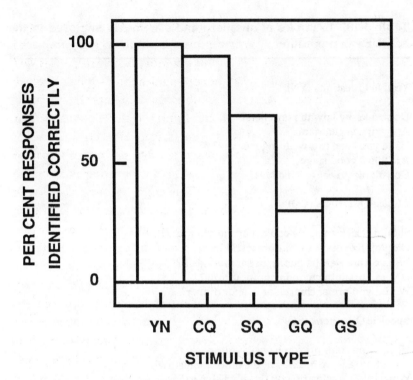

YN = Yes/No Question (e.g., "Are you afraid of worms?")
CQ = Choice Question (e.g., "Would you prefer soup or salad?")
SQ = Specific Question (e.g., "What year were you born?")
GQ = General Question (e.g., "Why do we have elections?")
GS = General Statement (e.g., "I like to ride my bicycle.")

Figure 4-3. Per cent of brief messages identified audio-visually by a severely hearing-impaired adult male (age 66). In each instance, the client spoke a prepared sentence of a particular type (see Table 4-18), to which the clinician responded appropriately (without repetition). The client's task was to identify these responses. Twenty examples of each type were presented.

Table 4-18. Examples of questions and statements employed in the ASQUE>>> procedure.

Yes/No Questions (YN)

Do you know how to play chess?
Are you a vegetarian?
Have you been to a wedding recently?
Are you a good singer?
Do you like to eat green olives?

Choice Questions (CQ)

Should I pack an apple or a banana in your lunch?
Did you fix your roof, or does it still leak?
Will you answer the phone, or should I get it?
Is your appointment today or tomorrow?
Would you prefer chicken or fish for dinner?

Specific Questions (SQ)

How many coins do you have in your pocket?
What time are we meeting at the office tomorrow?
Which radio station do you usually listen to?
How old is the big tree in your back yard?
Where's the pencil sharpener?

General Questions (GQ)

How can public transport be improved?
Why is this your favorite city?
How do you feel about camping in the mountains?
Why do so many people procrastinate?
How did they repair the air conditioner?

General Statements (GS)

My mother saves old Christmas cards.
This chair isn't very comfortable.
I always wear gloves when I work in the garden.
Some babies cry all the time.
My cat just had kittens.

We have constructed lists of questions/statements of various types for this purpose (see Table 4-18):

a. 50 questions that elicit *yes* or *no* responses;
b. 50 questions that incorporate two explicit response *choices*;
c. 50 questions that request *specific* information (the response topic is *limited* by the question);
d. 50 questions that seek *general* explanations, opinions, or feelings (the response topic is *specified* by the question);
e. 50 statements that describe, inform, or express opinions or feelings (the response topic is *suggested* by the statement).

We have applied these principles and related stimulus lists to communication therapy through a variety of interactive procedures, to be summarized in the following sections. This clinical practice may be carried out under auditory, visual, or combined auditory-visual conditions. During sessions, background noise or visual distractions may be introduced. In addition, a wide range of problem-solving techniques and clarification requests may be applied, as with the many other communication therapy procedures previously described.

---

1. *Con-sequence*

Goals: to help the client recognize that there are various general types of questions and statements (assertions); some types of stimulus utterance greatly limit the form and content of the "other communicator's" response (a function of the number of explicit/implicit alternatives), whereas other types of utterance limit the speaker's response only by topic; it usually is easier to understand responses which the speaker selects from a small set of given alternatives than responses which are only topically related to the hearing-impaired person's initiating utterance.

Procedure: The client presents successive sets of stimulus sentences from the printed ASQUE>>> lists, for example, 20 yes/no questions, 20 choice questions, 20 specific questions, and so forth*. The clinician responds appropriately to each question/statement in turn (e.g., stimulus: "When does the film start?"; response: "at 7:45"). The client repeats each response, and the clinician verifies correct perception. If communication difficulty occurs, both the client and the clinician apply clarification strategies until the client is able to identify the response. Following practice, both discuss how each type of stimulus question or statement can affect the intelligibility of the communication partner's response.

---

2. Con-tingent

Goals: to closely simulate the changing stimulus-response interchange that occurs in many real conversations; to help the client to develop a general awareness of the differences between (and the similarities within) particular question/statement types; to demonstrate some of the difficulties that can result from engaging in various forms of contingent-pair sequences; to allow the client to verbalize awareness of these sources of conversational dysfluency and thus become more conscious of the many complexities of interactive language.

Procedure: Numerous stimulus utterances of various types (e.g., 20 yes/no, 20 choice, etc.) are printed on small cards, one to a card. A similar number of blank cards (e.g., 20) also are included. The deck is shuffled and placed face down on the table. The hearing-impaired client takes each top card in turn and reads its message to the clinician, who responds appropriately to the verbal stimulus. When a blank card is drawn, this signals the *clinician* to take the *next* card and read *it* to the client (this brief role reversal is intended to simulate the loss of topic control in a

---

* In each of these practice activities, prior to actual spoken interchange with the hearing-impaired client, the clinician may introduce the task with printed ("full script") versions of the contingent-pairs.

conversation). In any instance, if communication difficulty occurs, both the client and the clinician apply clarification strategies as necessary until the client is able to identify the clinician's utterance. After each contingent pair interchange is complete, the client is required to place its stimulus card on one of two piles, labelled: "Difficult"/"Easy". Later, the client and clinician together discuss similarities between the cards in each pile, that is, what made them difficult or easy.

---

3. *Con-sider*

Goal: to demonstrate that stimulus questions/statements of different types often elicit responses that vary in intelligibility, but that the potential difficulties usually can be anticipated.

Procedure: The general procedure is similar to #2 (*Con-tingent*) above, but here, the hearing-impaired client is required to predict the difficulty of identifying the clinician's response to each question/statement *before* presenting the stimulus. That is, he/she first considers the potential difficulty of receiving a response to each item, and sorts the stimulus cards accordingly into "Difficult/Easy" piles. Then he/she presents the stimuli in each pile, attending to the clinician's contingent responses, to determine whether the predictions re intelligibility were accurate.

---

4. *Con(!)-parison*

Goals: to direct the hearing-impaired client's attention to those specific aspects of a question/statement which determine the potential intelligibility of the other communicator's response; to require the client to judge the likelihood of understanding the other communicator's response - prior to asking a question or making a statement.

Procedure: The clinician presents two question/statement stimulus cards (randomly selected) to the hearing-impaired client. The client compares these and indicates which utterance is likely to elicit the more intelligible response from a communication partner. He /she then presents each one, attends to the clinician's responses in each case, compares difficulties, and verifies whether his/her prediction was correct.

---

5. Con-descending

Goals: to help the hearing-impaired client become aware that a hierarchy of stimulus questions/statements exists, which may determine the difficulty of understanding the other communicator's response; to help the client learn to use lower-level stimulus utterances remedially.

Procedure: A list of printed general *statements* (GS) on various topics is prepared. When the hearing-impaired client presents one, the clinician responds appropriately. Following this response, the client is then requested to ask a descending series of *questions* related to the same topic: general (GQ), specific (SQ), choice (CQ), yes/no (YN). For example,
    "*I don't watch television very much.*" (original printed GS)
    "How do you feel about television programs ?" (client's GQ)
    "What kind of programs do you like to watch?" (client's SQ)
    "Do you prefer watching sport broadcasts or news?" (client's CQ)
    "Did you watch the 'Late Movie' last Saturday night?" (client's YN)
The clinician again responds to each one appropriately. If communication difficulty occurs, the client and clinician apply clarification strategies as required, until the client identifies each response, and this is verified. Following each sequence of five contingent pairs, the client and clinician discuss the relative difficulties of verbal interchange at the various stimulus levels.

---

6. Con-openers

Goal: to give the hearing-impaired client practice in generating conversation-opening stimuli of various types without the prompting provided by printed lists or stimulus cards.

Procedure: When requested, the hearing-impaired client is required to "open conversations" in various ways - as directed by the clinician, e.g., "Ask me a choice question about *grapefruit*."; "Now make a general statement about *shoes*." The clinician responds to each utterance appropriately. Clarification is provided as necessary until the client correctly identifies the response. In each case, the amount of time required by the client to construct and present each stimulus sentence is noted*.

---

7. Con-struct

Goals: To obtain a measure of frequency of occurrence of various types of initiating stimuli in real conversations. To help the clinician chart the client's progress in assuming control of conversations and manipulating them in structure (and/or content) to achieve conversational fluency.

Procedure: The hearing-impaired client and another person (e.g., friend, spouse, family member, clinician) conduct a brief conversation (see TOPICON, pp. 75-85). This may be recorded on video tape. The clinician or an observer tallies the types of initiating utterance spoken by the hearing-impaired person during this time (e.g., using the code: YN, CQ, SQ, GQ, GS). The frequency of occurrence of each type of conversation opener employed is calculated and graphed. The results are discussed with the client, in relation to the proportion of time taken for clarification, to overall fluency during the conversation, and to the judged level of conversational "satisfaction" (see pp. 187-197).

---

* In all these practice activities, the clinician or an observer may record the amount of time required to complete each contingent-pair interchange, using this as an estimate of conversational fluency.

We have found that the variety of ASQUE>>> procedures described above can be extremely useful in helping our hearing-impaired clients quickly become aware of the many factors that can affect ease of message reception and thus conversational fluency. We also find that this approach, incorporating self-discovery and analysis rather than didactic instruction, leads to rapid learning as well as retention of the many problem-solving (problem-avoidance?) principles.

Adaptive Approach to Conversation

As the result of our clinical experiences with several variants of TOPICON (pp. 75-85), QUEST?AR (pp. 124-129), and ASQUE>>> (pp. 129-138), we have begun to examine the specific methods by which hearing-impaired adults conduct successful conversations. It has been apparent that some of our clients exhibit personal *adaptive* strategies to achieve fluency. That is, a hearing-impaired person's choice of utterance seems to be (un)consciously influenced by (a) the intelligibility of, and also (b) the information conveyed by, his/her communication partner's previous utterances.

For example, when a particular hearing-impaired person presents a general question or statement, he/she may not be able to understand the elaborate description or complicated question that his/her communciation partner provides as a response. Clarification requests and strategies usually follow. The hearing-impaired person may adapt to the disruptive effects of this clarification by asking more *restrictive*, response-limiting questions, such as "yes/no" or other "forced-choice" types. Although these very directive questions yield responses that are nearly always intelligible, they limit the rate at which information and feelings can be exchanged. As a result, the hearing-impaired communicator may react to the tedium of experiencing a series of small successes by returning to ask *less* restrictive questions, or by making statements again, regardless of the consequences.

Thus, the stimulus-response level at which a hearing-impaired person comfortably participates in a conversation may fluctuate - depending on the relative proportion of recent successes and difficulties and also on the

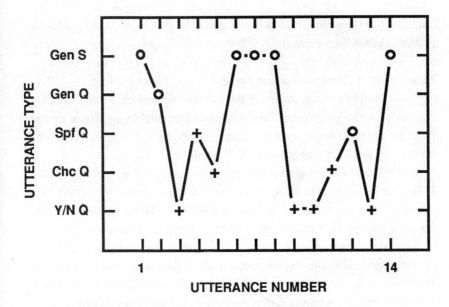

Figure 4-4. One person's adaptive approach to conversation. Data obtained from a 3-minute excerpt from a conversation about "antique furniture", between a severely hearing-impaired female (age 47) and her clinician. A *plus* (+) indicates that the client identified her communication partner's response without difficulty. A *circle* (O) indicates that the client required clarification of her communication partner's utterance before she could identify and respond to it.

rate of information flow (see Figure 4-4). An individual may even adopt a personal "threshold " - a balance between minor receptive difficulties and small successes - and attempt to maintain conversation at this comfort level, relying mainly on "specific" questions for example.

Many hearing-impaired people seem to be unaware of this adaptive approach to conversation. They either dominate others by talking continuously, withdraw from human interaction, or repeatedly place themselves in communicative jeopardy by attempting to converse in a "normal" way, with little thought given to the type or difficulty of responses that they elicit from others.

Mis-match of Communication Style

Most people are not aware of the subtle patterns of interaction that exist within their conversations*. This is reasonable, as many of the patterns become apparent only as the result of applying a particular theoretical point of view to a set of clinical data.

For example, during practice with ASQUE>>> materials (pp. 129-138), a severely hearing-impaired client (N.C., female, 63 years) was asked to present a list of 10 printed statements one-at-a-time to a communication therapist (e.g., "At my daughter's wedding, all the bridesmaids wore *yellow* dresses!"). Just before the clinician responded to each prepared statement, an observer (NPE) interrupted and asked the client to anticipate what the clinician's utterance was likely to be. Then, after the clinican responded, the observer asked the client, "What did she say?", and also, "Were you (almost) correct?"

Analysis of a transcript indicated that the hearing-impaired client expected *questions* as responses to her statements 8 times out of 10 (e.g., "What kind of flowers did they carry?"), although the clinician persistently responded with *elaborative statements* 10 times out of 10 (e.g., "The bridesmaids at *my* wedding wore light green!"). That is, although the clinician maintained a consistent (unplanned and unprompted) personal pattern of response throughout the session, the hearing-impaired client exhibited little awareness of this tendency and did not modify her overriding pattern of expectation. Moreover, she was able to (audio-visually) understand only 1 of the clinician's 10 utterances. This is not surprising, considering that she was expecting a completely different form of response. Individual interviews of the participants after the session revealed that: (a) the *client* had not become aware of the clinician's consistent response pattern; and (b) the *clinician* had not become aware

---

* Some notable exceptions include: politicians, psycho-therapists, novelists, teachers, and sales representatives.

Table 4-19. Examples of discrepancies between expected and received responses in conversation.

A speaker may:

a. expect an answer to a question, but receive another question instead:

   Hearing-impaired client said: "Would you like to go out to dinner with us?" (expected response: "Yes" or "No")

   Communication partner actually responded: "Where are you going?"

b. expect acknowledgement of, or (dis)agreement with, an assertion, but receive elaborative statements instead:

   Hearing-impaired client said: "The light's awfully dim in here!" (expected response: "Yes, it is!")

   Communication partner actually responded: "I can't see the menu very well. The print isn't very large, either!"

c. expect topic maintenance, but experience topic shift:

   Hearing-impaired client said: "That meal was really good, but the *Himalaya's* still my favourite restaurant!" (expected a comparison between restaurants)

   Communication partner actually responded: "But *you're* such a wonderful cook! You know I love your salads! Who would have thought of mixing broccoli, apricots, and sunflower seeds..."

of the client's consistent communicative expectations. Similar incompatible communication styles are likely to exist between other people as well (see Table 4-19). If the interactive styles of frequent communication partners (e.g., husband-wife, brother-sister, teacher-student) are *very* dissimilar, then their conversations might be seriously disrupted on a regular basis - perhaps by arguments as well as by routine attempts at sentence-clarification (see Watzlawick, Bavelas, and Jackson, 1967; Okun and Rappaport, 1980). These communication breakdowns could be especially common if one (or both) of the communicators also were *hearing-impaired*. This concept - disparity between communicators in conversational *style* - is not only a general pragmatic notion that invites further investigation but also appears to be a specific clinical communication problem that requires an effective remedial technique.

SUMMARY

In this chapter, we have described several perception-oriented therapies that are traditionally applied in aural rehabilitation, such as listening and lipreading practice, and have pointed out their potential benefits and practical limitations. We also have surveyed the various ways that situational, interpersonal, and sequential contexts can contribute to accurate reception of spoken messages. Language-use strategies incorporating syntactic and semantic components were suggested to help fill any remaining "perceptual gaps", and numerous examples were provided. Various pragmatic and problem-solving approaches to communication therapy also were introduced. We have found two conversation-based procedures (QUEST?AR and ASQUE>>>) to be especially effective tools, and have described several applications of each technique.

5

COMMUNICATION PARTNERS

Friends and family members often are the hearing-impaired person's principal communication partners. Most adults with aquired hearing losses learn compensatory strategies primarily through verbal interaction with these people, who serve as the focus for daily conversations. Consequently, friends and family members are in a unique position to contribute significantly to conversational fluency, and clinicians generally recommend that they play active roles in the rehabilitation process (Hull, 1982; Webster and Newhoff, 1981).

INTELLIGIBILITY

Communication involves the transfer of ideas from one person to another, usually by means of a common, or at least overlapping, linguistic code. Not all of the messages that one produces, however, are perfectly received. We may think of *intelligibility* as the proportion of an intended message that a receiver identifies (and comprehends) correctly.

Many factors can influence the intelligibility of a spoken message. For

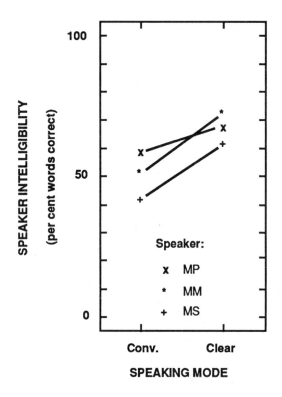

Figure 5-1. Intelligibility differences between "conversational" and "clear" speech. Three talkers recorded lists of brief sentences, speaking "normally" and "carefully" at different times. Five hearing-impaired adults listened to these recordings, and attempted to identify the items. Results from all listeners are pooled (after Picheny, Durlach, and Braida, 1985).

example, we know that people vary considerably in the acoustic *clarity* with which they produce speech. Their speech may differ in voice pitch and intensity, duration of segments, syllable stress, insertion of pauses, and/or the rate at which syllables are produced (Picheny, Durlach, and Braida, 1986) (see Figure 5-1). Their visible mouth and lip positions and their facial movements also may differ - the result of anatomical variations as well as many of the speech-related variables listed above (Kricos and Lesner, 1982).

We commonly refer to the low or high intelligibility of a person's *speech*, but intelligibility ultimately depends on much more than the speaker's vocal and articulatory attributes. For example, if the speaker desires to communicate with minimal effort, the spoken *message* must be: (1) semantically consistent (i.e., realistic in word and phrase associations); (2) syntactically simple (i.e., uncomplicated in word order); (3) pragmatically appropriate (i.e., expected at that particular point in the conversation); and (4) sufficiently brief (i.e., easily remembered). That is, the nature of the *message* and the *clarity* with which it is uttered both are important determiners of intelligibility (Figure 5-2).

Normally, speakers *listen* to themselves while speaking and rely on this acoustic feedback to determine whether the content and clarity of their messages were as they intended. Many speakers also survey the surrounding environment for any potential disruption from ambient noise or other distractions, and they may compensate by slowing syllable rate, increasing voice level, inserting pauses, or maximizing articulatory precision (Garber, Siegel, Pick, and Alcorn, 1976; McCall, 1984).

The *speaker*, however, does not possess complete control over successful transmission of a spoken message. For example, if the two communicators do not share components of a common language, then of course it is virtually impossible to obtain high message intelligibility. A speaker cannot cause an utterance to be intelligible if the person who receives the message has neither the linguistic competence, intellectual capacity, nor the life experiences to accurately reconstruct and appreciate the ideas that are expressed.

When a *hearing-impaired* person attends to someone's speech, he/she may not perceive all parts of the spoken message correctly (Evans, 1983). That is, the set of linguistic symbols that the person *receives* (perhaps through distorted hearing and/or lipreading) may be very different from the sequence that the speaker *produced* (and clearly heard) in the original message. In short, speech intelligibility depends not only on the message content and on the speaker's vocal and articulatory precision,

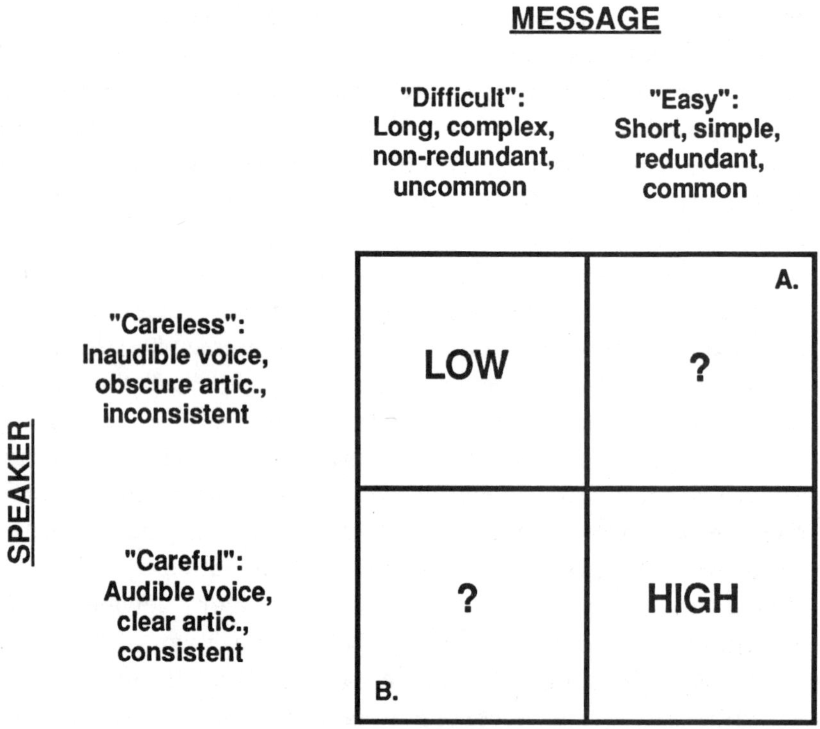

MESSAGE

	"Difficult": Long, complex, non-redundant, uncommon	"Easy": Short, simple, redundant, common
"Careless": Inaudible voice, obscure artic., inconsistent	LOW	? A.
"Careful": Audible voice, clear artic., consistent	? B.	HIGH

SPEAKER

Figure 5-2. Potential for message reception as a function of message content and speaker characteristics. A careful talker may be able to salvage "difficult" material, but a careless talker may cause even "easy" material to be seen/heard with uncertainty (i.e., spoken language is "filtered" through the person who produces the utterance). Under conditions A and B, message reception probably will depend on many other factors also, such as the hearing-impaired person's linguistic abilities and general knowledge, as well as the overall situational/conversational context.

but also on who is looking and listening (Carney, 1986).

Let us restate these points in a familiar context. A woman may speak with precise articulation and carefully controlled vocal patterns, but her hearing-impaired husband may not respond consistently or appropriately, regardless of her apparent verbal competence and his recognized facility with language. As a result, she (and he) may become confused, frustrated, and even angry. She may not realize that her intelligibility at any given moment will be *low* if her utterance is too long, is too complicated syntactically, is filled with perceptually difficult speech units (e.g., consonant blends), or is not expected by her husband. To summarize, one's *intelligibility* can vary considerably, depending: (1) (most obviously) on articulatory precision, vocal patterns, and the surrounding environment; (2) (less obviously) on the structure and content of the utterances; and (3) (least obviously) on the perceptual abilities, linguistic background, and interests, experiences, and expectations of the person for whom the messages are intended.

CLARITY

Nearly all adults speak with sufficient clarity to conduct ordinary conversations with other *normal-hearing* people. Most speakers, in fact, have little need to develop clarity that is greater than this. Clinical experience suggests, however, that without *specific* instruction and/or practice, many people never learn to speak clearly and carefully enough to be understood by *hearing-impaired* people (Mason, 1939; Pesonen, 1968; Kricos and Lesner, 1982). Some individuals do develop highly intelligible speech - without special instruction - but unfortunately, few also become the friends or relatives of a hearing-impaired person. Instead, it seems that many normal-hearing people are quite unaware of their careless verbal habits and must *learn* special methods for success in verbal communication (Picheny, Durlach, and Braida, 1985, 1986; Mohay, 1986).

STEPS TO SUCCESSFUL COMMUNICATION

Successful verbal communication with a hearing-impaired adult is a special skill, composed of several components. Simply stated, the communication partner:

a. sincerely wants to communicate with the hearing-impaired person;

b. recognizes that person's interests, and discusses these, or introduces topics that will interest the hearing-impaired individual;

c. participates in patterned "conversations", that is, rule-governed exchanges of ideas or feelings that include turn-taking;

d. employs appropriate eye contact, facial expression, posture, and gesture as complements to speech, and also acknowledges the hearing-impaired person's non-verbal cues as integral parts of the conversation;

e. forms messages in simple linguistic terms and speaks clearly, with successful speech communication (high intelligibility) a conscious goal;

f. confirms that spoken messages were received as they were intended;

g. applies a range of preparatory and remedial communication strategies, when necessary, to maintain or repair conversations; responds to clarification requests by the hearing-impaired person to maintain or modify conversations;

h. judges his/her interpretation of clarification requests made by the hearing-impaired individual; judges the success of each attempt at clarification;

i. responds to the hearing-impaired person's expressed desire to change topic; comfortably modifies conversational content and style to match a new interest; or introduces a different, more appropriate topic.

Most experienced *clinicians* learn these steps to successful communication with hearing-impaired adults after many years of interactive experience. With little effort, they can select words for easy identification, and can construct sentences that are linguistically simple. Moreover, they know how to clarify their speech and language patterns when misunderstandings occur. Most friends and relatives of hearing-impaired people also acquire a similar repertoire of basic communication skills after many years of verbal interaction.

SOME OBSTACLES

Friends and relatives of hearing-impaired people may learn these skills very slowly, however, because:

a. a speaker cannot see his/her own mouth while speaking, and thus cannot accurately judge its *visible* characteristics;

b. a speaker cannot hear his/her own speech as the hearing-impaired person hears it, and thus cannot accurately judge its *acoustic* qualities;

c. a speaker may receive intermittent or misleading feedback from the hearing-impaired person regarding his/her vocal patterns, articulatory clarity, and language use.

In general, learning through trial-and-error (and/or -success) can be a very slow and inefficient process - especially when the feedback regarding one's performance is provided inconsistently. Friends and relatives of a hearing-impaired adult often must wait until that person gains sufficient experience and confidence to accurately describe the effectiveness of their verbal communication strategies.

Enquiring friends and relatives may try to learn a set of *rules* for communicating easily with the hearing-impaired person (Kaplan, 1982; McCall, 1984). For example, it is well known that certain speech sounds may be acoustically indistinguishable to a hearing-impaired listener, such as /m,n/ or /i,u/ (Erber, 1972; Hack and Erber, 1982). Certain visible speech articulations look alike to a lipreader, such as /p,b,m/ or /f,v/ (Jeffers and Barley, 1971). Long words (e.g., *blackberry*) are potentially more intelligible than are short ones (e.g., *pen*), either through lipreading or through impaired hearing (Erber, 1971, 1981). Short, redundant, and linguistically simple descriptions of contextually appropriate topics tend to be the easiest for one to understand (e.g., "The bees flew to their hive." or "Worms live underground.") (Feier and Gerstman, 1980; Kalikow, Stevens, and Elliott, 1977). Background noise or reverberation (echo) in a room can seriously disrupt one's ability to perceive speech, even through hearing aids (Nabelek and Pickett, 1974; Finitzo-Hieber and Tillman, 1978). Briefly stated, the rules are: speak carefully; employ multi-syllabic words in short simple sentences; relate messages to the immediate context; indicate topic (shifts); and avoid distractions.

Regardless, friends or relatives who are aware of all these important factors still may be hard to understand. Why? There are many potential sources of difficulty. They may not be aware of how they *look* or *sound* to someone with a hearing impairment, who must lipread and listen to distorted sound qualities. They may misjudge the difficulty of particular words and sentence structures. They may forget to periodically *confirm* whether they have communicated successfully. In short, what they have learned and now "know" about successful communication may not be reflected in their typical verbal behaviour.

In addition, the *hearing-impaired* adult may not be aware of the relation between someone's speech and language habits and his/her own personal difficulties (or ease of understanding). Until this knowledge is acquired and consciously applied, the hearing-impaired individual can provide little to help the communication partner contribute to conversational fluency.

Most experienced communication therapists already know what the friends and relatives of a hearing-impaired adult need to learn about speech intelligibility and communication strategies. Unfortunately, many experienced clinicians, who are excellent *models* of verbal interaction, are unaware of their own special communication habits, instead conversing and applying remedial strategies intuitively. After many years, they have learned which conversational techniques are effective for communication with their hearing-impaired clients and which are not. Because they tend to apply these strategies without conscious analysis, however, they may not be able to describe to others precisely what they do or why they do it. An equally experienced, trained observer often is required to point out, describe, and interpret their successful communication acts, or refer to a sequence of conversational segments on videotape to illustrate a clinician's exemplary communication behaviour.

COMMUNICATION SKILL LEARNING

Observation by Oneself and Others
How can friends or relatives quickly learn the special verbal skills that

may be necessary to communicate fluently with a hearing-impaired adult? Observing oneself in a mirror while speaking, although commonly used for assessing the visibility of speech articulations, is not a very productive method (see Pflaster, 1979). When people practice in this way, it is easy for them to overestimate their potential for intelligibility, because they already know the message they are producing. Of course, during an actual face-to-face conversation, one cannot use this feedback technique anyway.

Normal-hearing communicators also may choose to *listen* carefully to themselves, in an attempt to estimate personal speech clarity (see Picheny, Durlach, and Braida, 1985). For the same reasons as those cited above, however, speakers probably will not judge their own acoustic speech patterns very harshly. Without listening through special electronic apparatus, friends or relatives are unlikely to ever hear their own speech as the hearing-impaired adult hears it - at a distance, affected by room noise and reverberation, passed through hearing aids, and changed in quality by impaired ears.

Alternatively, one may practice communicating with a trained normal-hearing or hearing-impaired observer, who can provide useful insight about one's voice, articulation, and visible appearance. For example, a very experienced speech pathologist or teacher can offer numerous suggestions to increase a speaker's clarity.

Special training incorporating role-playing, observation, and direct feedback often is used to develop clear verbal communication skills among radio and television newsreaders, actors, air-traffic controllers, politicians, telephone operators, and other professional speakers. In these cases, an experienced instructor listening in a realistic environment attends to samples of the talker's speech, evaluates these, and provides explicit guidance. Specific suggestions are given to the talker on how to increase clarity to expected groups of listeners (e.g., an audience of consumers, pilots, or voters) (see Figure 5-1).

SIMULATION, OBSERVATION, AND FEEDBACK

General Procedures

In our clinical programme, we employ similar training methods as described above, but in our work, the speakers are the hearing-impaired person's close friends and relatives, the messages are excerpts from their daily conversations, and those who provide instructive feedback are other normal-hearing people simulating hearing loss. We rarely use (video) tape recordings for practice (Sims, 1982,1985). Instead, most sessions rely on live interaction. While one person simulates hearing impairment, another learns how to verbally communicate various types of messages.

One aim is to allow participants to hear speech as it might be perceived by hearing-impaired people. Direct, airborne transmission of the speaker's utterances would invalidate this illusion. Therefore, the communicators sit in two separate rooms that are remotely located so that each participant cannot hear the other directly, that is, so that the simulation is not confounded by direct perception of speech sounds through the air or through walls*. The apparatus in these two rooms is joined by audio and video cables (Figure 5-3).

During each session, the speaker, in Room 2, sits before a television camera whose lens is adjusted to produce a life-sized head-and-shoulders image on the screen of the television monitor in Room 1. The speaker talks to the camera lens as if it were a pair of eyes (some talkers place a photo of the hearing-impaired person above the lens, if they cannot easily imagine this). A microphone mounted beside the television lens detects and delivers acoustic speech signals to a nearby audio pre-amplifier and variable filter, which represents a hearing aid. Both the video output of the camera (analogous to someone's eyes) and the audio

---

* We have tried using an audiometric test room with an observation window to separate the two communicators, but even those rooms with double walls and double glazing do not acoustically *isolate* them. A small amount of (low-frequency) speech energy usually is audible, transmitted through the walls, door, and/or window.

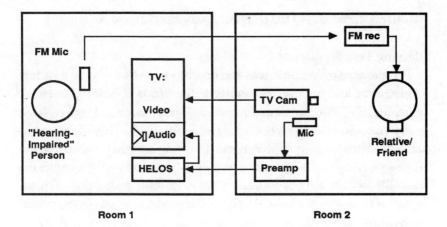

Figure 5-3. Block diagram of apparatus used in hearing-loss simulation.

output of the amplifier (analogous to a hearing aid) are conveyed through cables to the "hearing-impaired" person in Room 1.

The "hearing-impaired" individual sits before a television monitor in Room 1, on which the friend's or relative's image appears. Audio signals from Room 2 are fed into an electronic hearing-loss simulator (Gagne and Erber, 1987). These modified sounds are emitted via the television's audio system and loudspeaker. A wireless microphone, held by the "hearing- impaired" person, is used to transmit speech to an FM receiver and earphones in Room 2. This arrangement enables feedback and instruction to be delivered to the speaker (see Figure 5-3). To summarize: The communicators sit in two separate rooms, so that each person cannot hear the other directly (Figure 5-3). The (simulated) "hearing-impaired" person in Room 1 may ask a question or make a request. The friend/relative in Room 2 responds while facing a television camera and microphone. The "hearing-impaired" person in Room 1 *sees* the speaker's life-sized facial image on a television monitor and *hears* a distorted acoustic signal from its loudspeaker. The "hearing-impaired" person attends carefully, repeats the parts of the spoken message that were understood, analyses receptive errors, and makes informed requests for increased clarity. The speaker in Room 2 modifies his/her speech and language as necessary to achieve intelligibility.

Hearing-Loss Simulation

For many years, audiologists and educators have employed a variety of electronic techniques to demonstrate the effects of hearing loss (e.g., Villchur, 1974, 1978; Erber and Zeiser, 1974; Abraham and Stoker, 1984; Fabry and Van Tassell, 1986; Gagne and Erber, 1987). These demonstrations have given listeners with normal hearing a unique opportunity to experience how one might perceive speech through ears that change the audibility and quality of sounds. Usually, after friends, relatives, students, or clinicians have simulated "hearing loss" and have experienced many of the difficulties associated with impaired auditory-visual speech perception, they are highly motivated to increase their own speech clarity and thus make their verbal interaction with hearing-impaired people easier.

Apparatus

The electronic hearing-loss simulation system that we use, called "HELOS"* (Figure 5-4), can produce a wide range of auditory thresholds and amounts/types of supra-threshold distortion. The effect of an abnormal *threshold* (inability to hear low-intensity sounds) is created by directing the electrical speech signal through a circuit which does not pass weak energy. The percept of auditory *distortion* (inability to hear audible speech sounds clearly) is created by subjecting the electrical signal to random phase shifts, which are progressively greater for higher input frequencies (Gagne and Erber, 1987). Acoustic speech intelligibility can be varied from 0 to 100%, requiring the "hearing-impaired" person to increase/decrease the amount of visual attention directed to the speaker's face for lipreading cues.

---

* Apparatus manufactured and distributed by HELOSONICS, 12 Cook Street, Abbotsford, Victoria 3067, Australia.

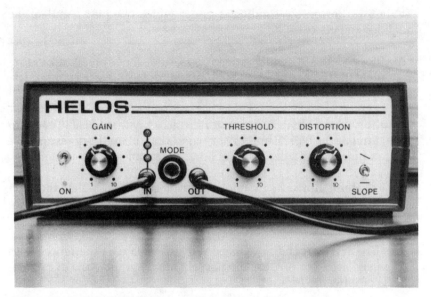

Figure 5-4. The "HELOS" hearing-loss simulation system.

We often set the ("aided") *threshold* level so that one cannot detect weak speech sounds or unstressed syllables, and we set the distortion level so that one can understand only about 10-20% of *audible* speech (i.e., some fragments of sentences still can be identified by listening alone). Sometimes, we increase the threshold or distortion settings beyond these levels - to make *auditory* perception of speech even more difficult and thus provide special *auditory-visual* practice to the person who is simulating hearing loss.

With HELOS, the listener also can experience sound patterns which are analogous to the sensations of *profound* hearing impairment. After high-frequency energy in the talker's speech is removed, its syllable pattern is extracted and is used to control the level of a vowel-like sound. By this process, all frequency-varying information is removed. The (simulated) "profoundly hearing-impaired person" hears a buzzing sound whose bursts convey the speaker's vocal pattern (see Erber, 1972; Gagne and Erber, 1987).

Table 5-1. Perceptual conditions under which one may simulate the qualities and effects of hearing loss.

* **Auditory-visual** (listening to distorted sound while lipreading): to simulate the typical bi-sensory conditions of face-to-face communication.

* **Auditory-alone** (listening to distorted sound without visible cues): to simulate the typical uni-sensory conditions of auditory assessment auditory habilitation, or telephone communication.

* **Visual-alone** (lipreading without acoustic cues): to simulate the typical uni-sensory conditions of lipreading assessment, or face-to-face communication with absent or malfunctioning hearing aids.

Note: The first two conditions listed above also may be experienced with *background noise* present, to help participants appreciate the disruptive effects of unwanted sound.

General Method

Each participant takes turns attempting to verbally communicate various types of messages, while another participant simulates hearing impairment and provides feedback and encouragement. Communication partners typically work together for about 6-8 weeks. Various perceptual conditions are employed (Table 5-1).

Most friends and relatives of our hearing-impaired clients prefer to assess the intelligibility of speech and language that *they* employ in their daily conversations. Consequently, we usually practice with samples of conversation (words, phrases, sentences) that they submit themselves. Their learning and application of principles in the "real world" is surveyed through weekly discussion and examined by means of a questionnaire (Table 5-7) and an interview.

Vowels and consonants

We have found that some speakers need to practice producing exemplary *visible* mouth shapes or generating speech elements with standard *acoustic* qualities. We use sets of vowels (spoken in /b/-V-/b/ context) and consonants (spoken in /a/-C-/a/ context) for this purpose. After the speaker presents each item, the "hearing-impaired" person repeats what was perceived. Either the speaker or an observer records responses on a matrix (see Erber, 1982; Gagne and Erber, 1987). Later practice is directed to correcting persistent, often idiosyncratic, articulatory deviations.

Words

We rarely employ items from word lists commonly used for audiometric assessment (e.g., AB Lists; PBs; NU-6 Lists). The words contained in those lists have been selected primarily on the basis of the specific speech sounds that they contain. Many of the items are uncommon and have little relevance to everyday communication (e.g., *hutch, beck, yearn*). Instead, we tend to employ lists of words compiled by close friends or relatives (Table 5-2) - because these people want to determine how easily frequently-spoken items can be identified through listening, lipreading, or auditory-visual perception.

Sentences

Participants also prepare lists of sentences for presentation during sessions, including statements and questions that they might typically speak during an ordinary day. These may include: descriptions, opinions, feelings, attitudes, or points of view (see Table 5-3a,b,c). *Questions* have ranged from those requiring limited responses ("Would you prefer toast or cereal this morning?") to less restrictive types ("Why is the rake by the back door?"). We also have collected other common question forms for presentation.

We have found that the contents of *yes/no* questions (Table 5-3b) tend to be difficult to identify. There seem to be several reasons: the sentences usually begin with a verb fragment (an auxiliary verb such as *is, do, did, have,* or *would*) and a pronoun (such as *this, that,* or *you*), both of which rarely receive vocal stress; the word order is inverted from that appearing in the more basic statement form; and the question's intent is conveyed partly by rising intonation.

Table 5-2. List of 200 commonly spoken nouns, compiled and submitted as practice material by the wife of a hearing-impaired client.

ant	clothesline	grapes	office	smoke
apple	coat	grapefruit	orange	soap
back	coffee	grass	pants	spider
bag	comb	gun	peach	sponge
banana	computer	hair	pear	spoon
bathtub	corn	ham	peas	stamp
beach	cup	hamburger	pen	steak
beans	curtain	hammer	pencil	stomach
bed	desk	hand	photo	store
bee	dish	handkerchief	picture	strawberry
beer	dog	handle	pie	street
belt	dollar	hat	pillow	supermarket
bicycle	door	hole	pin	table
bird	dress	house	postcard	tea
blanket	dryer	ice cube	potato	television
book	ear	ice cream	program	theatre
boots	earring	job	puddle	thumb
bowl	egg	juice	purse	ticket
box	eggplant	knife	radio	toe
bread	elbow	lake	ring	tomato
briefcase	envelope	lamp	roast beef	tooth
broccoli	eye	lawn	roof	toothbrush
bus	field	lawnmower	rope	toothpaste
bush	filing cabinet	leg	rubber	towel
butter	finger	lemon	rug	toast
butterfly	fingernail	letter	sandwich	tree
button	fish	lettuce	scarf	truck
cake	floor	light	scissors	typewriter
calculator	flower	lip	screen	umbrella
camera	folder	lunch	screwdriver	vegetable
can	foot	magazine	sewing machine	wall
can opener	football	match	shampoo	wallet
car	fork	milk	sheet	washing machine
carrot	fridge	mud	shirt	wasp
cat	frog	music	shoe	watch
chair	fruit	nail	shower	water
chicken	garden	news	sign	watermelon
clock	glass	newspaper	sink	window
cloud	glasses	nose	skirt	wine
clothes	gloves	number	sky	wrist

Table 5-3. Examples of (a) statements, (b) Yes/No questions, and (c) content-eliciting questions that have been presented during communication practice.

---

a. Statements

I've already typed most of the letters.
It's too hot to mow the lawn today!
I'll take your coat to the cleaners.
Your mother's coming over later for a short visit.
We've just bought a new washing machine!
The office closes today at 5:30.
We'll have to call a plumber to fix the toilet.
The exam papers blew all over the floor.
Her cat tried to climb through our bedroom window.
The post office is only three blocks away.

b. Yes/No questions

Are they going to help you build the fence?
Do you think that it's going to rain tonight?
Will you be working at the store on Saturday?
Is he still in the kitchen washing dishes?
Did you remember to pack your razor and shaving cream?
Were they very annoyed when you arrived so late?
Would you like another cup of coffee?
Do you have the sport section of the newspaper?
Do you want some ice cream for dessert?
Would you like to go to a movie tomorrow?

c. Content-eliciting questions

Where did you put my new gardening gloves?
What time does the party start tonight?
How many pieces of toast would you like?
When will they deliver your new dining table?
How much did you pay for your new vacuum cleaner?
What sort of dressing would you like on your salad?
How often do you go to the dentist?
What kind of dishwashing liquid do you use?
Where did you go camping last weekend?
When are you going to the vegetable market again?

Conversations

Communication partners are given numerous opportunities for active conversational interchange. For example, at particular times, the clinician will establish a realistic situation, topic, and purpose, and the participants are asked to simulate a conversation (see Davis and Wilcox, 1985; TOPICON: pp. 75-85). The setting might be the home, office, or factory, and the topic for conversation might be "pruning rose bushes", "Friday night shopping", "the new filing system", or "repair of refrigeration compressors". For fluent conversation, both communicators must be able to imagine and/or re-create familiar life situations and conversational patterns. This role-playing can be simplified by partly re-creating an appropriate environment for the communicators - e.g. with pictures, realistic objects, or recorded background sounds (see pp. 81-85).

We also frequently employ many of the same discourse materials that form a major part of our clinical communication therapy programme, such as QUEST?AR (pp.124-129) and ASQUE>>> (pp. 129-138). In each of these interactive procedures, speakers are able to practice the skills needed for fluent conversation.

Roles

At different times, friends and relatives *receive* speech as hearing-impaired people would, and they also practice *producing* easily understood speech and language. Thus, there are two complementary goals for each participant: (1) to learn about the effects of hearing impairment on communication; and (2) to acquire vocal, articulatory, and language-use strategies that can be used to enhance intelligibility.

During practice sessions, the "hearing-impaired" person learns to carefully *analyse* any auditory or visual difficulties, to *describe* them, and to *request* appropriate clarification (see pp. 116-124). For example, rather than saying, "Pardon?", or "I don't understand!", the "hearing-impaired" person can respond much more specifically, such as: "Please talk a little more slowly.", "That last sentence was too long for me.", "Your voice level dropped at the end.", "Did you say, 'The wall was..... *papered*?' ", or "Could you say the *last* three words again, please?". If the "hearing-impaired" person perceives only *nonsense* via lipreading or impaired hearing, then he/she is required to repeat the utterance as it was perceived (e.g., "my vad eats ahkee.....") so that the speaker can appreciate the way that the message looked and sounded (see Davis and Wilcox, 1985). The speaker carefully analyses the "hearing-impaired" person's response in planning the next communication attempt (e.g., in this case, the first and third words were perceived correctly). In consideration of this information, the speaker might apply more stress to the second syllable of the second word or eliminate an intruding lip movement preceding the fourth word.

When one plays the "hearing-impaired" person's role, he/she must not be self-conscious about responding with such nonmeaningful sequences. This explicit feedback regarding the perceived pattern can be very helpful to the speaker. As the speaker, one must shed personal sensitivity to direct verbal feedback and consider any helpful suggestions for modification of speech or language that are received from the "hearing impaired" person. That is, the speaker needs to emotionally separate one's vocal patterns from one's "self-image", and not react to the communication partner's suggestions as if they were *personal* criticism.

Clarification Strategies

Speakers can apply a variety of speech and language strategies to clarify their production of speech units, words, and/or sentences if at first they are not understood (see Erber and Greer, 1973; DeFilippo and Scott, 1978; Owens and Telleen, 1981; Erber, 1982, 1985; McCall, 1984) (also see pp. 116-124). Lists of alternative strategies, including brief descriptions and examples of each, are provided to each person upon entry to the programme (Tables 4-12 and 5-4).

Our emphasis on identification and remediation of communication difficulties closely resembles that of the Tracking Procedure (DeFilippo and Scott, 1978), but in these clinic sessions, we employ *conversational* rather than textual material, we typically do not count words nor time the duration of sessions, and the principal learner is the *speaker*.

Table 5-4. Some ways to enhance *visible* cues for speech.

---

* Increase contact duration of /m/ and /n/ to distinguish them from /p, b/ and /t, d/ respectively. Do not speak with excessive effort while producing /b/ or /d/, or they may appear as /p/ or /t/ (or even as /m/ or /n/, depending on the speaker's personal articulatory style).

* Place tongue between upper and lower teeth to clarify /ð, θ/.

* Spread lips, clench teeth firmly, and grin to indicate /s, z/.

* Bite lower lip with upper teeth to indicate /f,v/.

* Move jaw downward briefly while producing /k,g/.

* Shrug shoulders briefly during inspiration preceding /h/.

* Increase or decrease height/width of the lip aperture while producing extreme vowels, such as /i, æ, a, ɔ, u/.

* Increase duration of central vowels, such as /I, ɛ, U, ʌ/.

* Emphasize transition and contrast to clarify diphthongs /oI, ju, aI, aU, eI/.

* Speak a little more slowly than usual.

* Include all important speech articulations.

* Pause before and after key syllables, words, or phrases.

When the speaker fails to transmit a given message successfully, the "hearing-impaired" person usually will judge the reason for communication breakdown (e.g., wasn't paying attention; speaker's voice level too low; speech too rapid; sentence too long) and then suggest an appropriate remedial strategy based on this analysis of the problem (e.g., say it again; talk louder; speak more slowly; repeat the first part). The choice and application of these particular speech or language-use strategies are frequent subjects for later discussion - especially remedial methods that were found to be unusually effective or ineffective. Participants experiment freely with various communication strategies during sessions. If a specific clarification strategy can be identified as the reason for successful transmission of a message, then this is noted and pointed out to the speaker, if he/she is not already aware of the occurrence.

At first, most normal-hearing speakers experience great difficulty judging their own speech clarity (and thus their intelligibility) . As a result, they must initially rely on their "hearing-impaired" communication partners for feedback - regarding voice, articulation, visible appearance, and message complexity (see Owens and Telleen, 1981). After these early learning experiences, however, a typical normal-hearing speaker will assume anticipatory/corrective control, as the goal is independent communication with a real hearing-impaired person, who may not be willing or able to provide such specific guidance.

To achieve fluent communication, the "hearing-impaired" person must *correctly* identify any sources of communication difficulty and then request/apply appropriate clarification strategies. For example, if one judges articulation or voice to be inappropriate, he/she may ask the speaker to increase *clarity*. If linguistic complexity is considered to be the problem, the speaker may be requested to change the *structure* of the message. If the amount of contextual information is felt to be insufficient, the speaker may be required to provide additional *information* or (verbal) prompts. Through repeated practice, most speakers eventually learn to *anticipate* their "hearing-impaired" communication partner's difficulties - and to select vocabulary, maintain adequate voice level, articulate precisely, insert pauses, and speak slowly in their *initial* presentations. Some experienced speakers can describe many of these acquired anticipatory strategies in detail, but others are less aware of the subtle improvements that occur in their verbal behaviour.

Organization of Sessions

Participants usually take part in these hearing-loss simulation activities while their hearing-impaired friends or relatives are in concurrent communication therapy sessions. In other instances, a parent may attend while a hearing-impaired child attends speech/language development sessions. Small groups often are formed for efficient communication practice. In our experience, the optimal group size is about 2 or 3 people, plus a trained clinician who attends and organizes all sessions.

During a session, each participant usually is able to practice communicating with every other member of the group - either as the talker or as the "hearing-impaired" person. If a particular group contains more than two members, the extra participants may act as observers and notetakers (see Figure 2-3)*. In this role, they usually do not interact with either communicator. The *clinician*, however, frequently guides both participants during sessions, suggesting materials and strategies and also providing encouragement.

A typical one-hour session is organized as follows:

1. The clinician briefly reviews the previous week's activities, discussing the materials used, unusually easy or difficult items, and successful strategies, and then accepts each participant's written assignment (e.g., "Prepare a list of 50 commonly-used two-syllable words.").

2. The clinician selects communication partners, explains how the materials will be used for practice, and then describes any special conditions (e.g., poor illumination) or procedures to be followed (e.g., construction of highly predictive sentences).

3. Several pairs of communicators practice interacting with one another via the hearing-loss simulation system (Figure 5-3). The roles of normal-hearing and "hearing-impaired" person are rotated. Each pair practices

---

* In general, *observers* sit to one side (in Room 2) as they carefully attend to the interaction of the participants. Most observers have claimed that in this position, where they can easily analyse both parts of the conversation, they often are able to devise potentially effective strategies more easily than either active communicator. They have suggested that both the special viewpoint and the lack of pressure to communicate contribute to development of this skill.

for about 15 minutes; 5-minute breaks are provided as positions are exchanged.

4. Group discussion follows, coordinated by the clinician. During this time, the participants talk about successful utterances, application of particular strategies, difficulties, unexpected confusions, clarity/obscurity of speaker articulation, preferences for specific types of practice materials, and any special insights regarding effective speech communication. They often present personal anecdotes related to the outcome of the day's session.

5. The clinician assigns "homework" in preparation for next week's session: e.g., "Create a list of 20 brief requests that you typically direct to your hearing-impaired friend/relative." or "Think about what you have learned during today's session, and try to apply this new knowledge in conversations during the next week.".

Transcriptions

As previously stated, if a communication group contains more than two people, those who are not personally interacting during a practice session usually will take "notes" as they observe. We often videotape the sessions as well, for later review.

An observer/notetaker usually records the following information: all of the "hearing-impaired" person's responses, including the sequence of clarification strategies that were requested; a brief description of the speaker's final strategy, that is, the one which was found to effectively convey the message; the relative contributions of acoustic and visible components to successful identification of each message; the amount of general effort required by each participant for successful communication.

Where *words* have been employed as the stimulus items, the written notes yield a sequence of error responses leading to each correct identification. Where *sentences* have been presented, the transcription shows the order in which each fragment of a sentence became intelligible. These transcriptions also have provided considerable insight into the beneficial/inconsequential effects of various remedial strategies on the intelligibility of particular messages (Table 5-5a,b).

The observer/notetakers also describe all "interesting events" that occur during a communication session, such as:

a. portions of words or sentences that are not audible (e.g., "..........new dress.");

b. articulations that are not visible (e.g., initial /k/, as in the word *camera*);

c. ideosyncratic articulations that consistently intrude in particular situations (e.g., the speaker tends to bite her lower lip when pausing, which looks like /f/ or /v/);

d. particular words or phrases that persistently look/sound alike (e.g., *"it is"* <> *"is it"*; *bean* <> *meat* <> *beet*)

e. particular words/phrases/sentences that are very easy (e.g., *knife, table*) or very hard (e.g., *sink, kitchen*) to identify;

f. a particular vocal pattern or articulatory style that causes spoken messages to be especially easy or hard to understand (e.g., a regional accent);

g. extreme reliance on either auditory or visible cues for message reception;

h. extreme effort required for successful interaction with a particular communication partner.

Sentence Perception in Segments

We have found that "hearing-impaired" people often perceive sentences in a fragmentary or disordered fashion, rather than in a conventional beginning-to-end sequence. In general, the most *audible* or *visible* part of a sentence tends to be identified first, followed (as the result of subsequent repetitions and clarifications) by portions that are more obscure. Often segments that come first in a sentence or that seem to be important linguistically (e.g., a noun phrase, or a verb phrase) are *not* among those first understood by the "hearing-impaired" person, especially if these phrases contain an uncommon word, a difficult consonant blend, or many unstressed syllables. For example, in most Yes/No questions, neither the subject noun nor the verb receives very much

Table 5-5. Examples of (a) some auditory-visual confusions and (b) some strategies that were found to be effective.

a.

"vinegar" —————— "fingers"   [typical errors]
"hairbrush" —————— "apron"
"shopping" —————— "jumping"
"It's a hot day!" —————— "Is it a hot day?"

"(Let's) go (to the) bank."   (   ) = inaudible and/or indistinct
"Shut (the) door. (It's) cold!"
"(Would you like to) help (me)?"
"(Put this in the) bedroom!"
"(He's my) husband!"

"You're too short to reach that shelf!"   [the first three words, which contain rounded vowels, all appear similar]

b.

"Would you like *some/a piece of* cheese?"   [either visible word/ phrase helps one to identify the difficult word, *cheese*]

"I think we should take an umbrella."   [a visible cue that an assertion follows]

Original presentation (perceived as):   "Can you eat for me?"
Simply repeated: "Can you eat for real?"
Precise articulation; head tilted: "Can you hear the phone ring?"
     (correct)

Original presentation (perceived as):   "_____bathroom."
Simply repeated: "_____ clean the bathroom."
Pause between phrases: "I think ..... I'll clean the bathroom."
Greater emphasis on first three words: "I *will* clean the bathroom."
Extreme emphasis on second word: "I *did* clean the bathroom."
Must substituted for *need to*:   "I *must* clean the bathroom."
     "Oh! -
     "I *need to* clean the bathroom!"
     (correct: note the order in which the words were identified)

articulatory emphasis, as in the sentence, "(Did you bring your) *radio?*".
As a result, some sentences become known in a nearly *inverted* order
(Table 5-5).

Changes in Verbal Behaviour

Throughout the course of practice, all participants are encouraged to
report any changes in their own verbal behaviour which seem to result
from their involvement in the hearing-loss simulation process. In
addition, at the end of each series of sessions, all participants are
requested to complete a brief questionnaire, outlining their general
impressions (Table 5-6).

As the result of interactive experience with hearing-loss simulation,
most participants have changed the way that they organize conversations with their hearing-impaired friends or relatives. For example, some
people now consider whether the topic and related vocabulary are likely
to be easily understood, either visually or through impaired hearing.
Others think about a particular utterance before (or after) producing it,
considering other methods for "saying the same thing a different way".

All participants have reported that their involvement in hearing-loss
simulation sessions has made them much more aware of the various
speech and language-use strategies that are available to clarify an utterance. They no longer rely on *repetition* or *exaggeration* for intelligibility.
They now attempt to maintain voice level throughout sentences, pause
briefly between important words or phrases, and use appropriate, expressive facial expressions. Moreover, they claim that they have become
much more conscious of the need for precise articulation when they
speak.

Friends and relatives also have indicated that playing both normal-
hearing and "hearing-impaired" roles has helped them to recognize how
their choice of specific *words* and *word-order* affects intelligibility. They
report that they now are able to select words which they have learned are
easier to identify - or, alternatively, they are able to apply one of the many
language-use strategies which they have practiced in simulated conversations.

Table 5-6. After a series of hearing-loss simulation sessions, each participant is asked to complete a questionnaire.

QUESTIONNAIRE

1. What have you learned during simulation sessions about your: typical voice pitch; typical voice level; production of speech sounds; visible mouth movements; choice of words; sentence length and complexity?

2. What else have you learned about your speech and language habits - from watching yourself on *video tape*?

3. During the simulation sessions, which of your speech and language habits frequently confused your "hearing-impaired" communication partner?

4. Which speech and language *clarification strategies* seemed to help you the most (as speaker)?

5. What *different* things did you learn about communication - in your role as: the speaker; the "hearing-impaired" person; the observer or notetaker?

6. What have you discovered about the way that a "hearing-impaired" person uses auditory and visual cues together for speech understanding?

7. Which communication-practice activities did you like best: common words; question-answer; conversations; etc. Why?

8. How have these sessions helped you in daily conversations with your hearing-impaired friend or relative?

9. What has your hearing-impaired friend or relative asked you about these communication-practice sessions? How have you described the sessions?

10. How long do you think each session should be? How many total sessions should a person attend to gain most benefit?

SUMMARY

Conversational fluency depends not only on the hearing-impaired person's perceptual, conversation-management, and problem-solving abilities, but also on his/her communication partner's clarity of speech and simplicity of message. Communication partners can learn to maximize their (potential for) intelligibility by speaking typical words and sentences while another normal-hearing person simulating hearing loss provides direct feedback regarding ease of message reception. With this approach, both participants can learn about the perceptual effects of acquired hearing loss, as well as a variety of preparatory/remedial strategies for successful auditory-visual communication.

6

NEW DIRECTIONS

PAST AND FUTURE

Hearing losses of various types and degrees are prevalent in most modern societies. In the increasing din of the industrialized world, it is becoming quite common for adults to acquire noise-induced hearing losses and to develop related communication difficulties (Lipscombe, 1978). Moreover, people are living longer, and many acquire hearing losses as they age (Maurer and Rupp, 1979). Despite these recognized trends, the fields of Communication Therapy and Adult Aural Rehabilitation still are not well-established clinical specialties, and relatively few hearing-impaired people receive needed assistance with their communication problems.

Progress has been uneven. During the past fifty years, researchers have devoted considerable time and effort to the development of hearing test apparatus and audiological test procedures. Recently, large-scale research support also has been directed to improving the design of hearing aids, and to increasing the precision with which use of these aids is assessed. As a result, we now are able to *describe* hearing loss and *prescribe* hearing aids more efficiently than ever before. Many people continue to experience difficulty in face-to-face conversation, however, even while listening through optimally selected amplification systems.

Interest in psycholinguistics has grown rapidly in the past thirty years, but most studies of verbal interaction have been *developmental* in nature - examining conversations between *children* and their parents or teachers. Relatively few research studies have described the communication patterns of *adults* - with or without hearing impairment. Moreover, little applied research has been undertaken to improve communication- assessment and communication-practice materials, communication therapy procedures, or methods for counselling adults with acquired hearing impairments. For many clinicians, the term "aural rehabilitation" still means little more than the provision of hearing aids and related services.

Some of these deficiencies in our clinical processes have existed for a very long time. University students continue to point out the many gaps and contradictions that exist within/between current adult aural rehabilitation models and clinical practice. Their relentless criticism is directed mainly to the materials and procedures that are available for assessing and enhancing verbal communication in hearing-impaired adults. The clinical approach described in this text was devised to overcome many of these deficiencies. We need much more applied research, however, if we hope to provide adequate guidance to all the present and future hearing-impaired members of society. We cannot continue to rely on electronic apparatus as the basis for "therapy". Ultimately, we must replace our faith in technology with confidence in *ourselves* as clinicians (see Jaynes, 1982; Erber, 1986).

In this final chapter, we will describe some persistent needs in the field of adult aural rehabilitation and will suggest some promising directions for future study. We propose little essential research that would require expensive electronic apparatus or specialist staff. Instead, most of our future work would simply require that we: precisely express our clinical needs; gain the courage to create new rehabilitation materials and procedures; direct the application of these newly created methods; carefully observe the rehabilitation process; make ongoing modifications based on trial-and-experience; collect relevant data; and clearly report the results (see Ripich and Spinelli, 1985).

PARTICIPATION IN COMMUNICATION THERAPY

Some people with significant audiometric hearing losses, who have obvious communication problems, express little interest in attending a communication therapy programme. There are many reasons (see Table 6-1a). For example, the hearing-impaired person may not recognize the existence of a communication problem, as close friends and relatives compensate by spontaneously applying appropriate clarification strategies (McCall, 1984; Hetu, Lalonde and Getty, 1987). Or, that individual may consider the effects of hearing loss to be relatively unimportant components of the natural ageing process. In other instances, however, the reasons may be somewhat more pathological: the hearing-impaired person may be afraid to acknowledge the effects of ageing, may wish to avoid revealing his/her persistent communication failures, may be unable to accept the responsibility for making personal decisions, or may be unable to accept help from *anyone* (even a clinician) - as the result of chronically low self-esteem.

Other people, with relatively minor hearing losses, who have no apparent verbal communication problems, may nevertheless request help from a communication therapist. There are many reasons for these occurrences also (see Table 6-1b). The person may want more information or desire counselling regarding hereditary, progressive, or noise-induced hearing loss - in order to minimize the anticipated effects on communication. Or, the person may experience communication problems that are not *obvious* - such as receptive difficulties in noise, in groups, or when listening to particular individuals. There also are other reasons. The client may be abnormally precise, compulsive, or neurotic, and concerned with accurate reception of every spoken word. Or, the person may attend sessions for various psycho-social reasons, desiring the companionship and sustained personal attention of the clinician. When any of these anomalous situations occurs, the therapist may want to examine the apparent reasons for attendance, and carefully plan sub-

Table 6-1. Participation in a communication therapy programme.

a. Some people with significant hearing losses choose not to attend therapy sessions. Why? They .....

* may already employ communication strategies competently and confidently

* may feel that their present hearing aids compensate adequately

* may consider hearing loss to be a natural part of the ageing process, and of low priority, relative to other physical disabilities

* may communicate regularly with only a few sympathetic friends and family members, who recognize their needs and assist in conversation when necessary

---

* may deny that they have a hearing loss; claim that all their difficulties are caused by the "mumbling" of others

* may be unwilling to accept responsibility for self-help, or for change in their communication habits

* may actively resist pressure to receive therapy (desire continued dependency on friends and family members)

* may be unable to accept help from others; fear exposing their communication difficulties to a therapist

* may feel that they are "too old" and that it is "too late" (i.e., believe that they can't be helped)

---

sequent patterns of clinical interaction. Clinicians generally agree that effective communication therapy requires that each participant assume an appropriate portion of responsibility and play his/her expected role (Yalom, 1980; Luterman, 1984).

One rarely conducts in-depth interviews with short-term clients. It is

b. Some people who do *not* have significant hearing losses choose to attend communication therapy sessions anyway. Why? They .....

* may experience communication problems resulting from subtle auditory distortions; notice communication difficulties with particular people, in groups, in noise, or over the telephone

* may be distracted or annoyed by tinnitus

* may want information; may anticipate progressive familial hearing losses and may be preparing for the future

* may want to avoid hearing loss from noise exposure; may desire advice and counselling

* may fear the existence of another, unrelated disability (e.g., senility)

* may want to assist the clinician and/or students in learning (!)

* may be lonely and desire social contact; may enjoy the attention and presumed sympathy they receive from clinicians

* may have personal problems that they want to relate to a therapist (but may require *psycho*therapy, rather than *communication* therapy)

* may be easily irritated by occasional confusions in conversation; may obsessively want to understand everything that is said; may be unreasonably concerned about life's discomforts

even less common to assess the many reasons for non-attendance at communication therapy sessions among the general (hearing-impaired) population. Consequently, many of the points mentioned in this section are speculative, as they are based on limited information. Nevertheless, to be effective counsellors, we need to understand which factors motivate the people whom we (might) assist.

SELF-ASSESSMENT OF COMMUNICATION DISABILITY

Conventional audiometric test results may not adequately predict one's requirements for communication therapy. Questionnaires and carefully conducted interviews also are necessary. People exhibit very different personalities and life styles. They vary greatly in their need for social contact and verbal communication. As a result, people differ in the degree to which they are disabled by hearing loss. Most clinicians believe that it is important to allow hearing-impaired clients to describe the effects of reduced auditory sensitivity and clarity on their lives and thus to personally assess the severity of their communication disabilities.

To receive appropriate help, clients must first describe their communicative strengths and weaknesses, and they must convey these personal observations clearly and concisely. For many years, clinicians have needed a brief and simply-worded questionnaire to assess the hearing-impaired person's changing attitudes toward his/her own hearing loss. The aim of self-assessment is to enable the *hearing-impaired person* to concisely describe how he/she feels about the hearing loss (a judgement based on life experiences). Of course, this personal opinion may have little relation to how the *clinician* rates the degree of disability (a judgement based on observations and the results of audiometric tests).

Ideally, the communication therapist would not need to carefully explain or interpret the intent or format of a questionnaire, its instructions, or the wording of specific items. That is, the client would easily comprehend the nature of the required reponse (e.g., rating, rank-ordering, short descriptive statements), and would be able to quickly complete the self-assessment.

The HHIE ("Hearing Handicap Inventory for the Elderly") (Ventry and Weinstein, 1983), referred to earlier in this text (pp. 48-52), fulfills many of these clinical requirements. With only minor changes in wording, this brief self-assessment questionnaire has been found very appropriate as a complement to observation and interview techniques. There is a continuing need for brief evaluation forms to obtain similar information from friends and relatives of hearing-impaired adults, as well as from parents of hearing-impaired children (see Newman and Weinstein, 1986; Alpiner and McCarthy, 1987; Hetu, Lalonde, and Getty, 1987).

SCREENING PERCEPTUAL ABILITIES

Communication therapists also need a simply-administered perceptual test battery to determine a client's potential for receiving and processing speech through auditory, visual, and tactile modalities (see pp. 61-74). An ideal set of screening tests would quickly establish a client's capacity for distinguishing among a range of basic speech components. The types of stimuli might include visible mouth shapes, acoustic intensity patterns, voice pitch contours, vowel formant frequencies, fricative spectra, and so forth. Additional tests would specify each person's susceptibility to interference from noise and reverberation, as well as from visible distraction. Still other perceptual tasks would assess the contribution of short-term memory for sequences of speech units received through the various sensory modalities.

It is likely that computer-generated stimuli and computer-controlled test procedures could be employed for many of these routine assessments of a hearing-impaired client's perceptual abilities (Sims, 1985). The test results would suggest whether, with *practice*, a particular hearing-impaired adult could expect to remain reliant on *perceptual* cues for communication, or whether that person would need to shift reliance to *language-use* strategies to achieve conversational fluency.

DESIGNING HEARING AIDS TO MINIMIZE PERCEIVED DISTORTION

Ears with significant hearing losses exhibit not only *loss of auditory sensitivity* but also *distortion* of the qualities of sounds that are heard. Most modern electronic hearing aids are designed primarily to make the sounds of speech louder and thus more audible to hearing-impaired people. Nearly all of these amplification devices also incorporate intensity-limiting circuits that are intended to protect the user from strong sounds that have been increased in level. Modern hearing-aid amplifiers can be manufactured that add relatively little distortion of their own as they accomplish these functions (Johansson, 1973).

Ears with serious sensori-neural (and perhaps even conductive) abnormalities, however, distort the received sounds in unusual ways

(Bailey, 1983; Evans, 1983). These unwanted changes to the incoming signal can make speech communication extremely difficult for the listener, especially in a noisy environment. Binaural hearing aids and those with directional microphones can reduce many of the disruptive effects of environmental noise (see Hodgson, 1986). Separating desired speech from noise can be difficult, however, when the disruptive sounds are other voices originating near the speaker.

Considerable research on hearing aids is in progress. Many hearing-impaired people prefer to listen to speech reproduced by hearing aids with extended low-frequency response (Punch and Beck, 1980). Reducing gain in the high frequencies also is recognized as a simple way of diminishing the amount of unwanted auditory distortion that a hearing-impaired person perceives (Murray and Byrne, 1986). Design objectives, however, have progressed beyond the stage of simply modifying the speech spectrum for maximum audibility with minimum perceived distortion. Increased attention is being given to "processing" speech signals for optimal presentation to the impaired ear, redistributing information within the cochlea according to its capacity (Johansson, 1966; Braida, Durlach, Lippman, Hicks, Rabinowitz, and Reid, 1979; Haggard, 1983).

ASSESSMENT OF LINGUISTIC SKILLS

There is a need for several simple tests of a hearing-impaired adult's ability to use language (see Wiig and Semel, 1984). The most desirable clinical tests would be brief, practical, and efficient screening devices which also would adequately sample a person's verbal behaviour. These ideal screening procedures would estimate a hearing-impaired person's knowledge of sentence structure, word association, and interactive sequences - that is, one's application of "syntax, semantics, and pragmatics". Test results might predict how well the client can interpret spoken messages that are incompletely perceived, for which he/she must fill gaps on the basis of familiar word sequences and relationships.

We have described one form of language-assessment (pp. 105-114), in which various samples of language are presented in the form of printed or spoken sentence frames (Hull, 1976). Particular types of perceptual difficulty are represented by the presence of silences (blank spaces) or word fragments. The client is required to fill the gaps (i.e., write or name the missing word/phrase/sentence). We presume that a hearing-impaired person's ability to perform these simple completion tasks depends on a wide range of linguistic abilities, and we speculate that his/her performance is closely related to the skills that are required to identify and comprehend similar sentence fragments during daily conversation. This notion needs to be verified, and other screening procedures developed to assess language facility in adults with acquired hearing losses.

ASSESSMENT OF META-COMMUNICATION ABILITY

We often want to know how well a particular hearing-impaired client can analyse an ongoing conversation and then discuss essential details of the interactive communication process. It should be possible to construct a clinical "test" to assess an individual's meta-communication ability.

Such a screening test might require the hearing-impaired person to answer a set of prepared questions about language and communication (similar to those asked of a beginning linguistics or phonetics student). Some typical questions might be: How are you able to guess the missing word in the phrase, "hot and .... water"? (semantically related words) How are you able to guess the missing word in the sentence, "The little boy fed .... cat."? (syntactic rules) How is the sentence, "The glass broke on the floor." (inanimate subject) different from the sentence, "The girl walked on the floor."? (animate subject) Why are the words, "knitting" (single viseme), "pad" (homophenous), and "seepage" (rare) hard for you to lipread? How might I respond if *you* asked the questions, "Do you own a lawnmower?" (yes/no) or "When do you usually arrive at work in the morning?" (a time); or if *you* made the statement, "We've planted radishes in our garden!" (acknowledgement/extension/question). The responses to a variety of such questions would help one estimate the hearing-impaired person's current level of linguistic awareness, and might help a clinician judge the potential value of conducting in-depth discussions of conversational difficulties and their remediation through meta-communication with that client.

EXTENSION OF META-COMMUNICATION ABILITY

Awareness of one's linguistic tendencies can be potentially beneficial in many ways, as a person's habitual patterns of language-use can influence his/her overall (communicative) behaviour (see Ellis and Harper, 1975). We frequently encounter hearing-impaired clients, however, who seem to have little experience in analysing and discussing the form and content of their conversations - that is, engaging in "meta-communication". This deficiency in linguistic self-awareness can be a major obstacle to our communication therapy programme. We try to overcome this potential problem at whatever level our clients feel comfortable and capable (see Dean and Howell, 1986). We may try any (or all) of the following approaches:

(1) *Describe*: for example, the clinician explains, "When two people talk to one another, they may talk about ... (a variety of topics), present different kinds of messages ... (statements, questions), and respond to one another within conversations ... (take turns, give/get information, discuss, gossip)";

(2) *Provide examples*: for example, the clinician presents excerpts from conversations - by means of contingent pairs or a half-script - to demonstrate various types of common communication sequences;

(3) *Observe* other communicators: for example, the client and the clinician watch videotaped samples of conversation, followed by discussions of their form, content, fluency, dysfluency, strategies, effectiveness, and so forth;

(4) *Role-play*: for example, the client and the clinician enact simulated situations and conversations; the session may be interrupted discretely by a second clinician, who points out and briefly discusses potential sources of difficulty when they occur.

Much has been written recently about the natural acquisition of meta-communication skill by children (Moerk, 1977; Hakes, 1980; Pratt and Nesdale, 1984). Children develop these cognitive abilities at different rates; some people never become fully competent. We need a variety of remedial methods to assist hearing-impaired adults whose degree of language awareness and control is low.

RECOGNIZING SOURCES OF COMMUNICATION BREAKDOWN

When a conversation loses its continuity, the hearing-impaired person needs to discover the source(s) of the disruption as quickly as possible and initiate steps to alleviate the problem. We have found that most hearing-impaired communicators can easily learn to identify *speaker* deviations, such as misarticulation, low voice level, or rapid syllable rate. Most also are able to recognize common *environmental* disruptions such as noise or glare. All these cues, typically conveyed by gross acoustic or optical patterns, appear to be perceptually available even to those with extreme hearing losses. General awareness of these disruptive factors often is learned through maturation, through participation in innumerable conversations, and through a lifetime of looking and listening experience. As a result, it usually is not difficult to teach a hearing-impaired adult how to recognize speaker carelessness or environmental distraction (with the exception of *reverberation*, whose presence may be overlooked).

In contrast, many hearing-impaired people find it hard to recognize conversational situations where their receptive difficulties result from *complex sentence structures* generated by the speaker, or where their problems evolve from *pragmatic/interactive factors* which reduce sentence predictability. That is, many hearing-impaired communicators seem not to notice either the complexity of particular spoken messages or the subtlety inherent in most human interaction. It is not known whether ageing or acquired hearing loss makes recognition of these socio-linguistic factors difficult, or whether this deficiency in language analysis is characteristic of most communicators.

We feel that it is important for a hearing-impaired person to be able to distinguish between receptive difficulties that result from the speaker's *voice* or *articulation* and those that result from the speaker's presentation of complex *message* structures. For example, a listener would gain relatively little by requesting a slower, louder, or more carefully articulated version of a sentence that contains numerous embedded clauses. In that case, it might be more efficient to request *simplification* of the spoken message.

One way to point out the various linguistic factors is to make extreme comparisons, for example, to contrast the syntactic complexity and semantic content of the more difficult sentence, "Why wasn't the enormous skyscraper crushed by the flaming meteorite?" (inanimate subject, passive verb, question, negative, inverted word order, rare words, uncommon event), with that of the simpler sentence, "The tired truckdriver drank a cup of coffee." (animate subject - verb - object sequence, frequently-used words, common occurrence).

We need a repertoire of clinical techniques to help our hearing-impaired clients accurately identify different degrees of sentence complexity or recognize conversational situations that tend to produce pragmatic difficulty. For example, planned auditory-visual experiences with sentence patterns of various types (emphasizing intonation, pause, and stress cues) may help a severely hearing-impaired person recognize complicated syntactic structures, even when the message content is unclear. Clinicians may describe or enact selected contingent-pair sequences to point out problem-prone interactive patterns, such as the *assertion-question* sequence. Noisy backgrounds can be employed to provoke the emergence of particular communication difficulties. Observing others conversing live or on videotape may be useful as well, especially when this activity is followed by a discussion of the conversational events.

THE COMMUNICATION PARTNER

Nearly all hearing-impaired people encounter dysfluencies or communication breakdowns during conversations with normal-hearing people. Sometimes a hearing-impaired person is able to successfully apply his/her (auditory-visual) perceptual abilities and linguistic knowledge to overcome the problem. Sometimes one can resolve the

difficulties by consciously applying the problem-avoidance and problem-solving strategies that have been learned as the result of a communication therapy programme. But at other times, all these recommended
and well-practised techniques do not succeed as expected, and the hearing-impaired person misunderstands the spoken message regardless -
often because the *other communicator* lacks knowledge of clarification
strategies, is not creative in their use, or is generally uncooperative (Table
6-2a,b) (see Lieth, 1972 a, b; Fehr, Dybsky, Wacker, Kerr, and Kerr, 1979;
Hetu, Lalonde, and Getty, 1987). If communication failure frequently
occurs at work or at home, and associates, friends, and family provide
little assistance, then the hearing-impaired person is likely to become
very unhappy, frustrated, angry, or depressed.

You and the hearing-impaired person have several alternatives for
coping with this situation:

(1) revert to practice with prepared conversations in the form of "half-
scripts", in which the client learns how to request help and how to ask
very directive questions, each of which greatly limits the communication
partner's range of reponses (e.g., "Will you be visiting your sister on
Saturday or *Sunday*?");

(2) re-orient the client's relatives and friends to the need for clear speech
and the timely application of clarification/exaggeration strategies (in
these cases, the clinician acts as coordinator, arranging counselling and
practice sessions - see Chapter 5);

(3) limit extended conversations to familiar communication partners
who are known to possess greater empathy, knowledge, and willingness
to comply with the use of clarification strategies;

(4) encourage participation in social clubs or organizations for hearing-
impaired people, where other (trained and experienced) communicators
are likely to speak clearly, apply special communication strategies when
requested, and exhibit patience and cooperation;

(5) work with others in established organizations to increase the general
level of awareness in the surrounding community. This can be done by
participating in promotional activities, such as "Deafness Awareness
Week", where one can prepare posters, articles, press releases, taped

Table 6-2. Degrees of cooperation in conversation

a. Different levels of assistance may be provided. For example, the communication partner:

* may *always* present clear speech and language in anticipation of communication difficulties - spontaneously in response to recognised problems, and also at the request of the hearing-impaired communicator; produces these desired behaviours in *all* conversational contexts.

* may be able to present clear speech and language in anticipation, spontaneouly, and on request - when *prompted* by the clinical surroundings; but may not produce these desired behaviours at other times.

* may be able to produce desired communication behaviours when the hearing-impaired person *requests* clarification in a specific manner, but may *not* employ clear speech and language at other times - in anticipation of difficulties or spontaneously when problems occur.

* may be able to *describe and discuss* clarification principles and strategies, but does not exhibit these desired speech and language behaviours.

* may be *unaware* of principles and strategies for producing clear speech and language; does not know clarification techniques or how to apply them.

interviews, and so forth. The following are typical aims of such activities:

(a) diminish community biases toward hearing-impaired people (such as persistently negative attitudes toward aged individuals or toward hearing-aid users) (see Livneh, 1982);

(b) organize short courses to prepare normal-hearing people for "rare events" - such as occasional communication with a hearing-impaired person;

(c) inform people how to speak slowly and clearly, and how to create sentences to achieve high intelligibility;

(d) increase the level of caring, tolerance, and patience in *all* (hearing and hearing-impaired) communicators.

b. **Maximum assistance may not always be provided.** For example, the communication partner:

* may mistakenly believe that he/she consistently presents speech and language with clarity, as all utterances *sound* intelligible when they are produced.

* is not *consciously* aware of most speech/language processes or communication difficulties; has developed strong habits of language use; has great difficulty developing *conscious* analysis and control of language.

* cannot easily *generalize* from familiar lists of clarification strategies to real communication situations (e.g., cannot identify a potentially difficult situation when it occurs or is about to occur in a conversation).

* believes that he/she *already applies* appropriate clarification strategies when required, but when communication difficulties occur, tends to overarticulate, increase loudness, speak monosyllabically, or engage in other potentially disruptive speech and language behaviours.

* believes that the hearing-impaired communicator is much more knowledgeable about the auditory disability and its effects; thus *he/she* should be the person who solves any conversational problems.

* may be unwillling to acknowledge or share responsibility for any communication difficulties that occur (e.g., believes that the hearing-impaired person does not pay sufficient attention or does not "try hard enough" during conversations).

* may want to dominate, control, or influence the hearing-impaired person; exploits personal superiority in speech communication as a method for acquiring or maintaining such power.

There is a great need for large-scale campaigns to increase public knowledge of hearing impairment, and to increase general awareness of the potentially serious implications of this disability for face-to-face communication. This new knowledge may lead people not only to prevent personal hearing loss, but also to contribute to fluency when they find themselves in conversation with hearing-impaired individuals.

THE CLIENT'S FAMILY AND FRIENDS - WHO'S RESPONSIBLE?

There have been instances where the hearing-impaired individual exhibits little personal interest in communication therapy, but a *normal-hearing* spouse, relative, or friend does request help and attends the clinic instead. Throughout a series of sessions, the friend or relative acquires information about hearing loss, practises conversation-clarification strategies, and participates in counselling - learning how to interact more easily with the person who is hearing impaired. These friends and family members may rapidly become skilled communicators, effectively applying the principles that they learn. If full personal growth is to occur, and normal relationships are to develop, however, the hearing-impaired adult ultimately must assume personal responsibility for his/her own welfare. This may eventually come about through self-discovery, through interaction with family members, or through guidance by a therapist.

The search for effective life strategies and their successful application depends on self-motivation, and this in turn depends on the hearing-impaired person's acceptance of responsibility. Frequently, other family members are very aware of their daily communication difficulties and actively work to overcome or avoid them. The hearing-impaired person may not be aware of, or acknowledge, the existence of these common communication problems - he/she may deny any personal responsibility for the discomfort of others. From one point of view, the hearing-impaired person is *not* responsible for their *discomfort* (that is a function of their reactions to stressful situations), but his/her hearing loss *is* responsible for the *conversational dysfluencies* that occur.

The hearing-impaired individual may deny that the communication problem is a personal responsibility, because the hearing impairment is not his/her *fault*. The person may express the attitude: "This hearing loss (and its consequences) is not *mine* - because I didn't want it; I didn't choose to acquire it." (see Kushner, 1981). That is, the person is unable to accept - as a part of life and self - the reality of the hearing impairment, its continuing existence, and its effects on verbal interaction. The person is unable to progressively and realistically modify his/her self image from that of someone who has appeared to be physically and communicatively intact to that of someone who now seems to be an "imperfect" version of his/her previous self.

Communication therapy and psycho-social counselling can help one to acquire greater understanding of self and the ageing process, leading the client to acknowledge the associated hearing impairment, accept responsibility for its consequences, and work to compensate for the disability. We need a wide range of effective counselling methods to assist our hearing-impaired clients through each of these stages of normal development (see Kushner, 1981; Luterman, 1984). We also need to incorporate courses in counselling into all our audiology, speech-language pathology, and special education programmes.

FLUENCY IN CONVERSATION

A "fluent" conversation is one in which information, ideas, feelings, and attitudes are exchanged in an efficient and coherent manner. Such a conversation contains few diversions, little explanation, definition, or clarification, and not very much "meta-communication". Although it is apparent that the ease with which one shares information, ideas, and so forth is strongly affected by the format of the conversation, the identity of the other communicator, and the surrounding environmental conditions (Erber, 1985), many other factors also contribute - such as one's attitudes, non-verbal skills, and use of frequent verification.

At present, there is no standard method for quantifying the "fluency" of a conversation, yet we have found that many experienced communication therapists can reliably judge the fluency of (live or videotaped) dialogue. We have noted, however, that although clinicians can easily and reliably rate what they observe on a scale of "fluency", "efficiency", or "naturalness", they have difficulty specifying the *bases* for their judgements. They claim that they consider numerous factors, such as: coordination of turn-taking (absence of silences, few interruptions); topic maintenance; and independent use of repair strategies. We have begun to incorporate these and other likely contributing factors into an assessment scale, similar to that proposed by Prutting and Kirchner

(1987) - in order to establish the conditions associated with conversational fluency (see Tables 3-11, 3-12).

One basic component of fluency appears to be the *efficiency* with which ideas and feelings are conveyed by the communicators, that is, the "rate of exchange" within the conversation. To assess fluency as defined in this way, one might count the total number of target words, sentences, or concepts successfully exchanged per minute - an approach similar to that employed in the Tracking Procedure (DeFilippo and Scott, 1978). Some other measures that have been proposed are: the time required to obtain answers to a set of questions (Erber, 1982); the time required to complete a half-scripted conversational sequence, such as that prescribed by QUEST?AR (Erber, 1985); or the time required to transmit a specific number of information-laden messages (see Yorkston, Beukelman, and Flowers, 1980; Erber, 1985).

Most clinicians agree that *conversational fluency* is likely to be judged "high" when each participating communicator uses approximately equal parts of the total conversation time for self-expression, and when turns are freely exchanged (but see Luterman, 1984). There also is general agreement that conversational fluency would be judged "high" when each communicator has no difficulty understanding the other, that is, when the proportion of time devoted to turn-taking repairs or to remedial clarification requests/strategies is low (Prutting and Kirchner, 1987).

After extensive observation of normal/abnormal conversations and also numerous interviews with hearing-impaired people and their communication partners, we have hypothesized that three basic factors are the principal correlates of judged "fluency": (1) the turn-per-minute rate; (2) the proportion of time that each communicator talks during the conversation; and (3) the proportion of total conversation time actually devoted to information exchange (and not to clarification or metacommunication).

The main advantages of this simple three-factor approach to describing conversational fluency are: (a) all variables are easily quantified: an

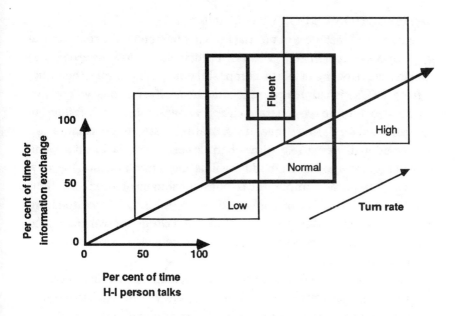

Figure 6-1. *Three-dimensional model* of "conversational fluency". A fluent conversation is one in which: (1) the turn rate is typical of natural, normal interchange; (2) the two communicators (hearing-impaired, normal hearing) share conversational talk-time nearly equally; and (3) most time is used for exchange of information, ideas, and feelings rather than for clarification or meta-communication.

observer requires only (a videotape of) the conversation and a stopwatch for timing various segments; and (b) the (hypothetical) results can easily be summarized and graphed (see Figure 6-1). Early, informal observations have suggested that this simple three-factor description is a reasonable approach to examining the concept of *conversational fluency*. Of course, we need to examine the reliability and validity of these notions. Assessment of conversational fluency is an interesting area that requires further observation and research.

SATISFACTION IN CONVERSATION

In nearly all instances of normal human interaction, the communicators hope to experience a sense of participation, close interpersonal contact, and a feeling of joint accomplishment. Stated simply, they want to feel *good* ("satisfied") during and after their conversations with others. We hope to develop the general concept of *"conversational satisfaction"* to complement existing measures, estimates, or correlates of conversational *fluency* (e.g., time-sharing; absence of clarification), and thus to provide another method for validating communication therapy. What perhaps is more important, is the establishment of those conditions which lead to feelings of conversational *satisfaction*. Once they are identified, we should be able to create *satisfied clients* (and also satisfied communication partners), which may ultimately lead to our own satisfaction as clinicians.

In general, to produce *satisfying* conversations, we first need to identify the major contributing factors. Then we can work systematically to obtain and provide these essential conditions.

We have examined a large number of simulated conversations between numerous pairs of normal-hearing adult communicators (in each case, one participant simulated hearing loss: see Chapter 5). Each conversation was observed by about forty speech-language pathology students, who had been trained in the theory and practice of this communication therapy programme. They all took extensive notes during their observations, discussed their findings, and contributed opinions regarding potential sources of satisfaction within the conversations.

Their judgements regarding likely sources of conversational satisfaction are summarized in Table 6-3. This list suggests that a wide variety of emotional needs and desired outcomes might affect the satisfaction that one derives from a conversation, such as feelings of progress, gain, spontaneity, and mutual understanding. We conclude that a large number of factors probably contribute to conversational satisfaction (but see Hecht, 1978b, who established only one major and two minor factors: "general affect/morale"; "substance/salience"; "free interaction").

This list of conversational conditions represents the cumulative judgement of many experienced observers who themselves are frequent verbal communicators. It is very likely that *all* these factors can contribute to satisfaction in daily conversation, but that each one is important in special ways to each communicator. That is, the sources of one's conversational satisfaction may be ideosyncratic, and related to one's own personal needs (Hecht, 1978a). If so, the relative importance of the various factors must be determined for each set of communication partners and conversational situation separately. This explanation seems likely, when we consider the many (sometimes contradictory) opinions that have been expressed by observers (e.g., preferences for familiar vs unfamiliar topics; few vs many silent intervals; few vs many digressions). We are likely to discover that the pleasure or satisfaction that people derive from conversation is a subtle variable - one that is not easily assessed by clinicians simply counting occurrences of particular verbal behaviours. Important contributing factors may be: the personal *relationship* between the communication partners (degree of "intimacy"); each participant's *expectations* and *purpose* for the conversation (see Table 6-4); and the *outcomes* of the conversation that result from sharing ideas and opinions (i.e., differences between attitudes and emotional states before and after the conversation) (Hecht, 1978a,b).

RELATION BETWEEN FLUENCY AND SATISFACTION

As previously stated, conversational "fluency" is a measure closely related to the *rate* at which information, ideas, and beliefs are transmitted by communicators. Fluency can be estimated accurately by an external observer, or through later analysis of a videotape of the conversation. If one of the active participants attempts to assess communicative fluency *during* the conversation, then the act of assessment is likely to disrupt his/her personal contribution to that fluency. In contrast, "satisfaction" is a measure of the *feelings* and attitudes of each communicator toward the way in which the conversation has progressed , considering his/her own personal (perhaps unconscious) reasons for communicating (e.g., positive expectation and fulfillment) (see Tables 6-3, 6-4).

Table 6-3. Some personal sources of "satisfaction" in conversation, as expressed by a large group of normal-hearing adults.
If one's *positive* expectations are fulfilled (or one's *negative* expectations are *not* fulfilled), then feelings of **satisfaction** usually result (Hecht, 1978). The following expectations for **conversation** have been expressed:

Temporal aspects / rhythm of interchange

* Each speaker will occupy an appropriate share of conversation time.
* Turn-taking will progress smoothly. There will be few interruptions or gaps. Occasional thoughtful silences, however, can be important.
* One's communication partner will know when to relinquish his/her turn.
* Little content will be predictable, but some ritual may be necessary when conversations begin or end.

Meta-communication / clarification

* The two communicators will possess overlapping linguistic competence.
* Each communicator will understand the other. Perceptual errors and cognitive confusions will be infrequent. Little conversation time will be devoted to repetition or clarificaton. (Yet, a communicator may be disappointed if he/she thinks that *no* clarification will ever be required, i.e., if one expects no confusions, contradictions, or challenges).

Topic

* One's communication partner will possess similar world knowledge and life experiences.
* The topic will be interesting.
* Abrupt digressions into new, perhaps related, topics will be infrequent. (Conversations, however, might be extremely boring and/or frustrating if the two communicators *always* maintained the topic, possessed identical knowledge, and agreed on everything.).

Intimacy / sensitivity

* The communication partner will understand one's thoughts and feelings.
* One will understand the *other* communicator's thoughts and feelings. (That is, a condition of shared intimacy will exist, where one's beliefs, self-worth, and conditions of existence will be verified. If a state of perfect understanding existed and *all* utterances could be predicted, however, there would be little need for overt conversation.).

Table 6-3 continued

Information

* One will acquire new information and/or obtain a new viewpoint.
* One will help the other to acquire information and/or obtain a new viewpoint.

Time / direction / fantasy

* Each communicator will help the other to recall shared ideas, beliefs, and experiences.
* Each communicator believes that the conversation has a purpose and a direction - progressing toward a (common ?) goal.
* Different objectives and points of view will be expressed, developed, and defended.
* The two communicators will mutually agree on a belief or a plan for action.
* One communicator will inspire the other to action.

Attitude

* One's communication partner will enter the conversation without conscious biases and without a disruptive attitude (e.g., re choice of topic or time available). Yet, another person's stong opinions can be interesting - to examine, criticize, or support.

Honesty

* One's communication partner will express "truth", or will distort/exaggerate in ways that are interesting, exciting, or humorous.
* One will enjoy the other communicator's company. The conversation will serve to bring them together for psycho/social/sexual contact. The conversation will provide (future) access to the individual for unexpressed, hidden purposes.

Power / control

* One will be able to dominate, overpower, or control the other - through logical argument, greater knowledge, subtlety, harassment, or voice level.
* One will be able to obtain advice, direction, or authority from the other, who is held in higher esteem than oneself.

Only a *participant* in a conversation can judge the personal satisfaction or pleasure that is derived from a particular unit of communication. If an external *observer* attempts to judge the satisfaction that the communicators derive from participating in a conversation, then inaccuracy is likely to result, because that observer may not share the conversational expectations of either participant. Moreover, an observer cannot avoid *projecting* his/her own general purposes and personal needs. That is, each participant or observer perceives the function of a conversation in terms of one's own purposes or goals, and so each individual will experience and judge it differently.

We are beginning to consider the relation between the fluency of conversations and the satisfaction that participants derive from the verbal interchange. Experience indicates that adults with normal hearing and good communication skills, whose conversations are judged to be very fluent, experience an extremely *wide range* of satisfaction as the result of such conversations. Their consequent emotional states, in fact, are observed to range from extreme depression to extreme elation, as the result of participation in *very fluent* conversations. Stated simply, a high degree of fluency enables one to conduct a wide variety of conversations. Some of these very fluent conversations will yield desired outcomes, but others will not.

In contrast, clinical observations suggest that adults with extremely poor hearing and limited compensatory skills (e.g., poor lipreading performance, inadequate conversation-management strategies) typically experience non-fluent (verbal) conversations. Because of their persistent difficulty in receiving or conveying even the most basic feelings or concepts, nearly all such seriously hearing-impaired individuals report that they obtain a very low level of satisfaction from participating in (non-fluent) conversations.

Many hearing-impaired people are more fortunate, however. Some have acquired less disabling hearing losses. Others successfully employ learned lipreading skills or language-use strategies to maintain fluency. Our observations indicate that hearing-impaired people vary widely in the ease with which they communicate verbally. Their conversations range in fluency from near-zero to near-normal levels. Consequently, their satisfaction will vary in like manner - from that experienced by a

Table 6-4. Some general functions of human communication (see Jakobson in Parret, 1971; Wiig and Semel,1984).

Establish/maintain orientation to reality:
Express memory, awareness, belief
Plan, imagine, speculate, fantasize, delude
Test, verify, or deny existence of self or self-worth

Establish/maintain social contact:
Associate with others
Establish identity, point of reference
Occupy time; alleviate boredom
Obtain group security, protection
Enact mating rituals
Develop societies, civilizations, history

Supplement direct sensory input:
Describe or narrate
Give or get information
Give or get direction, instruction
Classify things or events

Influence behaviour of others:
Give or get power, control
Give or get rewards, punishment
Compliment or ridicule
Inspire or deceive

Reveal or stimulate feelings/emotions:
Express joy, sadness, anger
Increase or decrease anxiety
Give or get sympathy, security, pleasure, "love"

Explore artistic possibilities:
Entertain - through humour, song
Write, read poetry
Write/enact drama

Express language awareness:
Analyse, compare, classify language acts
Discuss language, communication

---

person whose conversations are *non-fluent* to that experienced by someone whose conversations are *very fluent*. As explained before, this simply suggests that a hearing-impaired person with greater conversational fluency is permitted the *opportunity to experience* a wider range of satisfaction than one with virtually no conversational fluency. It does *not* mean that a hearing-impaired person with greater fluency will necessarily *obtain* a greater level of satisfaction from participation in conversations (see Figure 6-2).

We may present this point another way. Most clinicians would agree that the *opportunity* to derive satisfaction from a conversation depends on a minimal amount of fluency in the verbal exchange. The actual *level* of satisfaction obtained, however, depends on numerous subtle aspects of each communicator's personal goals and expectations - and on the outcome of the conversation in relation to those conscious or unconscious desires (see Table 6-5).

If these hypotheses reflect reality, what implications exist for the rehabilitation of hearing-impaired people? The acquisition of basic conversational fluency is a principal objective of our communication therapy programme. If we are competent clinicians, we can expect all our clients to become more *fluent* (as well as to become more "natural" and more "effective") communicators as the result of therapy. But the client's level of *satisfaction*, a somewhat independent variable, may *not* increase concurrently (unless increased *fluency* itself has been the client's primary therapeutic goal). Thus, it is not realistic to expect all our clients to become *happier* communicators as the result of a (successful) fluency-oriented communication therapy programme. Reaching that lofty goal awaits the devlopment of more sophisticated counselling, socio-linguistic, and psycho-therapeutic techniques. If our professional and personal *satisfaction* depends on our clients' conversational *satisfaction*, then we are likely to be repeatedly disappointed.

DIFFICULT CASES

Some hearing-impaired clients are difficult to treat, for various *non-auditory* reasons. This group includes: (1) people who compensate for their difficulties in speech perception by dominating conversations - and

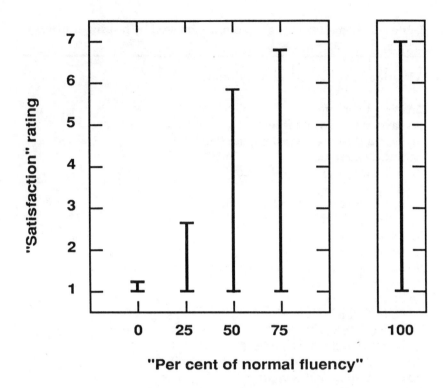

Figure 6-2. Hypothesized relation between (ranges of) communicator "satisfaction" and conversational "fluency". Fluency provides an *opportunity* for satisfaction, but does not *guarantee* it, as the occurrence of satisfaction depends on many other factors (e.g., fulfillment of expectations).

whose aggressive verbal behaviour is very difficult to modify; (2) people with extremely poor perceptual abilities who must request that speakers apply speech and language-use strategies, but who lack the assertiveness to obtain such help from others; (3) people who choose to avoid conversation in their personal lives rather than learn a repertoire of compensatory strategies via communication therapy; (4) people who have great difficulty acquiring meta-communication skills (i.e., for whom commu-

Table 6-5. Long-term life goals often expressed by hearing-impaired people.

A hearing-impaired person may want:

"to enjoy life more"
"to have more fun at parties"
"to have a closer relationship with family"
"to find a better job"
"to be a more independent person"
"to have more friends"
"to be better educated; to learn more"
"to be more self confident"
"to be happy"
"to be less tense"
"to be treated normally - not be patronized"
"to be more sociable"
"to be more successful in a job"
"to go out more"
"to be more secure"
"to be respected more by others"
"to see old friends more; to renew friendships"
"to enjoy family parties more"
"to get more pleasure out of club membership"
"to be a better student"

nication is something to *do*, but not something to *think* or *talk* about); (5) people who accept no responsibility for their own rehabilitation, blame everyone else for their difficulties, and who show little interest in therapeutic procedures; (6) people whose families exploit the hearing disability as a means for usurping power in the home; (7) people whose native language differs from that of the clinician, or whose cultural background impedes the client-clinician relationship; (8) people whose life goals and expectations extend beyond the capabilities of the communication therapist.

We need guidelines and effective strategies for resolving these and other professional dilemmas. We need more research on how to help difficult-to-treat clients and more open discussion of these (prevalent?) clinical problems.

IS CERTAINTY NECESSARY?

We often have heard our colleagues/ourselves say: "But we can't treat *that* problem!"; "We don't know enough yet!"; "We don't have the appropriate clinical experience!"; or "We haven't collected sufficient research data!" - just before referring a client to another expert who may be equally ignorant. It is an unfortunate fact that some hearing-impaired individuals do have *unique* personal and communication problems for which there are no well-practised clinical routines. Many other hearing-impaired people have *common* communication problems for which no simple clinical solutions have ever been developed. We frequently choose not to accept either type of client - probably because they require that we work too hard and be too creative. Moreover, neither their communicative progress nor our therapeutic "success" is guaranteed. Yet, if we accept these people as clients, attempt communication therapy, and achieve even moderate gains, a secondary result usually is a feeling of great personal and professional accomplishment.

All human transactions, including those of communication therapy, involve the elements of "risk" and "gain". We may ask, must we be *certain* of the therapeutic outcome before accepting a particular person for rehabilitation? In the case of a communication disorder that is difficult to treat in a conventional way, the clinician risks consuming (wasting?) considerable time and energy. But as a result, the communication therapist may gain a large measure of professional experience, as well as the positive feelings that come with success, such as mutual pleasure and increased self-esteem. Moreover, as is true of all people in nearly all situations, the communication therapist learns very little unless new interactive problems are confronted, the unexpected happens, and therapeutic errors occur - to be analysed later. No one makes significant progress in any profession as the result of routine and secure clinical experiences.

Table 6-6. Four types of clinical activity, distinguished by potential "risk" and "gain", with an example of each.

Low risk / low gain:
e.g., provide instruction in insertion of hearing-aid batteries, and in care of earmoulds to an elderly hearing-impaired person

Low risk / high gain:
e.g., teach a hearing-impaired person how to recognize several sources of communication breakdown, and how to apply appropriate clarification strategies

High risk / low gain:
e.g., provide auditory practice in distinguishing /f/ from /θ/ for a person with a severe high-frequency hearing loss

High risk / high gain:
e.g., develop meta-communication skills in a person who possesses little more than superficial understanding of human interaction

---

Clinicians have suggested that there are four main types of clinician-client relationship (Table 6-6). These can be described in terms of the potential "risk" and "gain" that are involved: low risk/low gain; low risk/high gain; high risk/low gain; high risk/high gain.

We derive much of our professional satisfaction from fluent verbal interaction with our clients. If they are "successful" with basic conversational tasks, we feel good. If we/they work extremely hard, and they overcome major obstacles in communication, we feel *very* good. We frequently devise client-acceptance criteria and communication therapy strategies with these simple contingencies in mind. We may welcome low risk/low gain tasks as they are known to be "safe", requiring very little planning, insight, or even conscious thought. We may *prefer* low risk/high gain clients, however, as the personal rewards for a measured degree of effort usually are greater for both communicators. Unfortunately, the many small pleasures that result from a series of low-risk clients are not necessarily cumulative. Because the professional rewards in these cases are somewhat automatic and thus predictable, their psychological significance tends to wane over time. That is, the magnitude of each positive feeling may diminish with each small clinical success. The long-term effect on the communication therapist may be disinterest, boredom, and ultimately even professional "burnout".

Regardless, clients who fit into neither low-risk category may often be ignored or referred to another professional. Very few therapists ever persist with high-risk clients. Some, however, have chosen to actively seek high-risk clinical interaction with hearing-impaired people who exhibit difficult communication problems. Attempting high-risk communication therapy, however, requires that the clinician possess certain personality characteristics, for example: a considerable amount of self-confidence; desire to accept a challenge; competitive tendencies; personal pride; interest in learning; a sense of humour; as well as willingness to appear foolish occasionally - while learning a new clinical skill in the presence of one's clients. Perhaps high-risk activities should be attempted only by *very experienced clinicians* (or perhaps only by *inexperienced students,* who usually are less concerned with their professional reputations). Either way, we must recognize that this rehabilitative field will flourish only when its members have the courage to explore new pathways to communicative and professional satisfaction.

REFERENCES

Aborn, M., Rubenstein, H., and Sterling, T.D. (1959). Sources of contextual constraint upon words in sentences. *Journal of Experimental Psychology, 57,* 171-180.

Abraham, S. and Stoker, R.G. (1984). An evaluation of methods used to teach speech to the hearing impaired using a simulation technique. *Volta Review, 86,* 325-335.

Alich, G.W. (1967). Language communication by lipreading. In *Proceedings of the International Conference on Oral Education of the Deaf.* Washington, DC: A.G. Bell Association for the Deaf, 465-482.

Alpiner, J.G. (Ed.) (1982). *Handbook of adult rehabilitative audiology (2nd ed.).* Baltimore: Williams and Wilkins.

Alpiner, J.G. (1987). Evaluation of adult communication function. In Alpiner, J.G. and McCarthy, P.A. (Eds.), *Rehabilitative audiology: Children and adults.* Baltimore: Williams and Wilkins, 44-114.

Alyeshmerni, M. and Taubr, P. (1975). *Working with aspects of language (2nd ed.).* New York: Harcourt, Brace, Jovanovich.

Argyle, M. (1975). *Bodily communication.* London: Methuen.

Bailey, P.J. (1983). Hearing for speech: The information transmitted in normal and impaired hearing. In Lutman, M.E. and Haggard, M.P. (Eds.), *Hearing science and hearing disorders.* London: Academic Press, 1-34.

Beagley, H.A. (Ed.) (1981). *Audiology and audiological medicine, Vol. 1.* Oxford: Oxford University Press.

Bedrosian, J.L. (1985). An approach to developing conversational competence. In Ripich, D.N. and Spinelli, F.M. (Eds.), *School discourse problems.* San Diego: College-Hill Press, 231-255.

Bentler, R.A. and Tyler, R.S. (1987). Tinnitus management. *ASHA, 29*, 27-32.

Berger, K.W. (1972). *Speechreading.* Baltimore: National Educational Press.

Berger, K.W. and Popelka, G.R. (1971). Extra-facial gestures in relation to speechreading. *Journal of Communication Disorders, 3*, 302-308.

Berko, J. (1958). The child's learning of English morphology. *Word, 14*, 150-177.

Bess, F.H., Freeman, B.A., and Sinclair, J.S. (Eds.) (1981). *Amplification in education.* Washington, DC: A.G. Bell Association for the Deaf.

Binnie, C.A. (1976). Relevant aural rehabilitation. In Northern, J. (Ed.), *Hearing disorders.* Boston: Little, Brown, and Company, 213-227.

Binnie, C.A. (1977). Attitude changes following speechreading training. *Scandinavian Audiology, 6*, 13-19.

Binnie, C.A., Jackson, P.L., and Montgomery, A.A. (1976). Visual intelligibility of consonants: A lipreading screening test with implications for aural rehabilitation. *Journal of Speech and Hearing Disorders, 41*, 530-539.

Blamey, P.J. and Clark, G.M. (1987). Psychophysical studies relavant to the design of a digital electrotactile speech processor. *Journal of the Acoustical Society of America, 82*, 116-125.

Bode, D.L., Tweedie, D., and Hull, R.H. (1982). Improving communication through aural rehabilitation. In R.H. Hull (Ed.), *Rehabilitative audiology.* New York: Grune and Stratton, 101-115.

Boothroyd, A. (1968). Statistical theory of the speech discrimination score. *Journal of the Acoustical Society of America, 43*, 362-367.

Braida, L.D., Durlach, N.I., Lippman, R.P., Hicks, B.L., Rabinowitz, W.M., and Reid, C.M. (1979). Hearing aids - A review of past research on linear amplification, amplitude compression, and frequency-lowering. *ASHA Monograph 19.*

Bunger, A.M. (1961). *Speechreading - Jena Method*. Danville, IL: Interstate Press.

Byrne, D. (1986). Recent advances in acoustic hearing aids. In Cole, E. and Gregory, H. (Eds.), Auditory learning. *Volta Review, 88* (Number 5: Supplement), 31-43.

Carhart, R. (1961). Auditory training. In Davis, H. (Ed.), *Hearing and deafness*. New York: Rinehart Books, 276-299.

Carney, A.E. (1986). Understanding speech intelligibility in the hearing impaired. *Topics in language disorders, 16,* 47-59.

Castle, D.L. (1980). *Telephone training for the deaf*. Rochester, NY: National Technical Institute for the Deaf.

Chermak, G.D. (1981). *Handbook of audiological rehabilitation*. Springfield, IL: Thomas.

Cherry, C. (1966). *On human communication (2nd ed.)*. Cambridge, MA: MIT Press.

Clark, H. and Clark, E. (1977). *Psychology and language*. New York: Harcourt, Brace, Jovanovich.

Clezy, G. (1979). *Modification of the mother-child interchange in language, speech, and hearing*. Baltimore: University Park Press.

Clezy, G. (1984). Interactive analysis. In Muller, D. (Ed.), *Remediating children's language*. London: Croon Helm, 85-112.

Clouser, R.A. (1976). The effect of vowel-consonant ratio and sentence length on lipreading ability. *American Annals of the Deaf, 121,* 513-518.

Cohen, G. (1987). Speech comprehension in the elderly. The effects of cognitive changes. *British Journal of Audiology, 21,* 221-226.

Cole, E.C. and Gregory, H. (Eds.) (1986). Auditory learning. *Volta Review, 88* (Number 5: Supplement).

Corso, J.F. (1977). Presbyacusis, hearing aids, and aging. *Audiology, 16,* 146-163.

Dance, F.E.X. (1967). Toward a theory of human communication. In Dance, F.E.X. (Ed.), *Human communication theory: Original essays*. New York: Holt, Rinehart, and Winston.

Danhauer, J.L., Garnett, C.M., and Edgerton, B.J. (1985). Older persons' performance on auditory, visual, and auditory-visual presentations of the Edgerton and Danhauer Nonsense Syllable Test. *Ear and Hearing, 6,* 191-197.

Danz, A.D. and Binnie, C.A. (1983). Quantification of the effects of training the auditory-visual reception of connected speech. *Ear and Hearing, 4,* 146-151.

Davis, H. and Silverman, S.R. (Eds.) (1978). *Hearing and deafness (4th ed.)* New York: Holt, Rinehart, and Winston.

Davis, G.A. and Wilcox, M.J. (1985). *Adult aphasia rehabilitation: Applied pragmatics*. San Diego: College-Hill Press.

Dean, E. and Howell, J. (1986). Developing linguistic awareness: A theoretically based approach to phonological disorders. *British Journal of Disorders of Communication , 21,* 223-238.

DeFilippo, C.L. (1982a). Memory for articulated sequences and lip-reading performance of hearing-impaired observers. *Volta Review, 84,* 134-145.

DeFilippo, C.L. (1982b). Tactile perception. In Sims, D.G., Walter, G.G., and Whitehead, R.L. (Eds.), *Deafness and communication*. Baltimore: Williams and Wilkins, 40-52.

DeFilippo, C.L. and Scott, B.L. (1978). A method for training and evaluating the reception of ongoing speech. *Journal of the Acoustical Society of America, 63,* 1186-1192.

Demorest, M.E. (1986). Problem-solving: Stages, strategies, and stumbling blocks. *Journal of the Academy of Rehabilitative Audiology, 19,* 13-26.

Denes, P.B. and Pinson, E.N. (1973). *The speech chain*. Garden City, N.J.: Anchor Press.

DiMatteo, M.R. and DiNicola, D.D. (1982). Practitioner-patient relationships: The communication of information. In DiMatteo, M.R. and DiNicola, D.D., *Achieving patient compliance*. New York: Pergamon Press.

Duncan, S. (1972). Some signals and rules for taking speaking turns in conversations. *Journal of Personality and Social Psychology, 23,* 283-292.

Duncan, S. (1973). Toward a grammar for dyadic conversation. *Semiotica, 9,* 27-47.

Eisenberg, L.S. (1985). Perceptual capabilities with the cochlear implant: Implications for aural rehabilitation. *Ear and Hearing, 6* (Number 3: Supplement), 60S-69S.

Ellis, A. and Harper, R.A. (1975). *A new guide to rational living*. Englewood Cliffs, NJ: Prentice-Hall.

Entwisle, D.R. (1966). *Word associations of young children*. Baltimore: Johns Hopkins Press.

Erber, N.P. (1971). Effects of distance on the visual reception of speech. *Journal of Speech and Hearing Research, 14,* 848-857.

Erber, N.P. (1972). Auditory, visual, and auditory-visual recognition of consonants by children with normal and impaired hearing. *Journal of Speech and Hearing Research, 15,* 413-422.

Erber, N.P. (1975). Auditory-visual perception of speech. *Journal of Speech and Hearing Disorders, 40,* 481-492.

Erber, N.P. (1981). Speech perception by hearing-impaired children. In Bess, F.H., Freeman, B.A., and Sinclair, J.S. (Eds.), *Amplification in education*. Washington, DC: A. G. Bell Association for the Deaf, 69-88.

Erber, N.P. (1982). *Auditory training*. Washington, DC: A. G. Bell Association for the Deaf.

Erber, N.P. (1985). *Telephone communication and hearing impairment.* San Diego: College-Hill Press.

Erber, N.P. (1986). Hearing aids: Their/our limitations. *Hearing Technology Review, 3,* 7-8.

Erber, N.P. and DeFilippo, C.L. (1978). A new method for assessing auditory-visual identification of sentences by hearing-impaired children (unpublished study). St. Louis: Central Institute for the Deaf.

Erber, N.P. and Greer, C.W. (1973). Communication strategies used by teachers at an oral school for the deaf. *Volta Review, 75,* 480- 485.

Erber, N.P. and Zeiser, M.L. (1974). Classroom observation under conditions of simulated profound deafness. *Volta Review, 76,* 352-360.

Eriksson-Mangold, M.M. and Erlandsson, S.I. (1984). The psychological importance of non-verbal sounds. *Scandinavian Audiology, 13,* 243-249.

Evans, E.F. (1983). Pathophysiology of the peripheral hearing mechanism. In Lutman, M.E. and Haggard, M.P. (Eds.), *Hearing science and hearing disorders.* London: Academic Press, 61-80.

Fabry, D.A. and Van Tasell, D.J. (1986). Masked and filtered simulation of hearing loss: Effects on consonant recognition. *Journal of Speech and Hearing Research, 29,* 170-178.

Falvo, D.R., Allen, H., and Maki, D.R. (1982). Psychosocial aspects of invisible disability. *Rehabilitation literature, 43,* 2-6.

Fehr, M.J., Dybsky, A., Wacker, D., Kerr, J., and Kerr, N. (1979). Obtaining help from strangers: Effects of eye contact, visible struggling, and direct requests. *Rehabilitation Psychology, 26,* 1-6.

Feier, C.D. and Gerstman, L.J. (1980). Sentence comprehension abilities throughout the adult life span. *Journal of Gerontology, 35,* 722-728.

Finitzo-Hieber, T. and Tillman, T.W. (1978). Room acoustics effects on monosyllabic word discrimination ability for normal and hearing-impaired children. *Journal of Speech and Hearing Research, 21,* 440-458.

Fisher, C.G. (1968). Confusions among visually perceived consonants. *Journal of Speech and Hearing Research, 11*, 796-804.

Franks, J.R. (1976). The relationship of non-linguistic visual perception to lipreading skill. *Journal of the Academy of Rehabilitative Audiology, 9*, 31-37.

Franks, J.R. (1982). Judgements of hearing aid processed music. *Ear and Hearing, 3*, 18-23.

Franks, J.R. and Beckmann, N.J. (1985). Rejection of hearing aids: Attitudes of a geriatric sample. *Ear and Hearing, 6*, 161-166.

Gagne, J.P. and Erber, N.P. (1987). Simulation of sensorineural hearing impairment. *Ear and Hearing, 8*, 232-243.

Garber, S.F., Siegel, G.M., Pick, H.L., and Alcorn, S.R. (1976). The influence of selected masking noises on Lombard and sidetone amplification effects. *Journal of Speech and Hearing Disorders, 19*, 523-535.

Gardner, H.J. (1971). Application of a high-frequency consonant discrimination word list in hearing-aid evaluation. *Journal of Speech and Hearing Disorders, 36*, 354-355.

Garstecki, D.C. (1981a). Auditory-visual training paradigm for hearing-impaired adults. *Journal of the Academy of Rehabilitative Audiology, 14*, 223-238.

Garstecki, D.C. (1981b). Aural rehabilitation for the aging adult. In Beasley, D.S. and Davis, G.A. (Eds.), *Aging: Communication processes and disorders*. New York: Grune and Stratton, 267-280.

Garstecki, D.C. and O'Neill, J.J. (1980). Situational cue and strategy influence on speechreading. *Scandinavian Audiology, 9*, 147-151.

Gerot, L. (1977). The role of kinesics in speechreading. *Australian Teacher of the Deaf, 18*, 51-58.

Goldstein, M.A. (1939). *The acoustic method.* St.Louis: Laryngoscope Press.

Goldstein, D.P. and Stephens, S.D.G. (1981). Audiological rehabilitation: Management model I. *Audiology, 20,* 432-452.

Goodwin, C. (1981). *Conversation organization: Interaction between speakers and hearers.* New York: Academic Press.

Grice, H. (1975). Logic and conversation. In Cole, P. and Morgan, J. (Eds.), *Syntax and semantics: Speech acts.* New York: Academic Press, 41-58.

Griffith, P.L., Johnson, H.A., and Dastoli, S.L. (1985). If teaching is conversation, can conversation be taught?: Discourse abilities in hearing impaired children. In Ripich, D.N. and Spinelli, F.M. (Eds.), *School discourse problems,* San Diego: College-Hill Press, 149-177.

Hack, Z.C. and Erber, N.P. (1982). Auditory, visual, and auditory- visual perception of vowels by hearing-impaired children. *Journal of Speech and Hearing Research, 25,* 100-107.

Haggard, M.P. (1983). New and old conceptions of hearing aids. In Lutman, M.E. and Haggard, M.P. (Eds.), *Hearing science and hearing disorders.* London: Academic Press, 231-282.

Hakes, D.T. (1980). *The development of metalinguistic abilities in children.* Berlin: Springer-Verlag.

Hardick, E.J. and Gans, R.E. (1982). An approach to rehabilitation with amplification. *Ear and Hearing, 3,* 178-182.

Hayes, D. and Jerger, J. (1979). Aging and the use of hearing aids. *Scandinavian Audiology, 8,* 33-40.

Hecht, M.L. (1978a). Toward a conceptualization of communication satisfaction. *Quarterly Journal of Speech, 64,* 47-62.

Hecht, M.L. (1978b). The conceptualization and measurement of interpersonal communication satisfaction. *Human Communication Research, 4,* 253-264.

Hetu, R., Lalonde, M., and Getty, L. (1987). Psychosocial disadvantages associated with occupational hearing loss as experienced in the family. *Audiology, 26,* 141-152.

Hochberg, I., Levitt, H., and Osberger, M.J. (Eds.) (1983). *Speech of the hearing impaired.* Baltimore: University Park Press.

Hodgson, W.R. (1986). *Hearing aid assessment and use in audiologic habilitation (3rd ed.).* Baltimore: Williams and Wilkins.

Hull, R.H. (1976). A linguistic approach to the teaching of speech-reading: Theoretical and practical concepts. *Journal of the Academy of Rehabilitative Audiology, 9,* 14-19.

Hull, R.H. (1980). Aural rehabilitation for the elderly. In Schow, R.L. and Nerbonne, M.A. (Eds.), *Introduction to aural rehabilitation.* Baltimore: University Park Press, 311-348.

Hull, R.H. (1982). Programs in the health care facility. In Hull. R.H. (Ed.), *Rehabilitative audiology.* New York: Grune and Stratton, 425-443.

Hurvitz, J.H. and Carmen, R. (1981). *Special devices for hard of hearing, deaf, and deaf-blind persons.* Boston: Little, Brown, and Company.

Iler, K.L., Danhauer, J.L., and Mulac, A. (1982). Peer perceptions of geriatrics wearing hearing aids. *Journal of Speech and Hearing Disorders, 47,* 433-438.

Jaynes, J. (1982). *The origin of consciousness in the breakdown of the bicameral mind.* Boston: Houghton-Mifflin.

Jeffers, J. and Barley, M. (1971). Speechreading (lipreading). Springfield, IL: Thomas.

Johansson, B. (1966). The use of the Transposer for the management of the deaf child. *International Audiology, 5,* 362-372.

Johansson, B. (1973). The hearing aid as a technical-audiological problem. *Scandinavian Audiology, Supplement 3,* 56-76.

Kalikow, D.N., Stevens, K.N., and Elliott, L.L. (1977). Development of a test of speech intelligibility in noise using sentence materials of controlled word predictability. *Journal of the Acoustical Society of America, 61,* 1337-1351.

Kaplan, H.F. (1982). Facilitating adjustment. In Hull, R.H. (Ed.), *Rehabilitative Audiology.* New York: Grune and Stratton, 81-100.

Kapteyn, T.S. (1977a). Satisfaction with fitted hearing aids: An analysis of rather technical information. *Scandinavian Audiology, 6,* 147-156.

Kapteyn, T.S. (1977b). Satisfaction with fitted hearing aids: An investigation into the influence of psychosocial factors. *Scandinavian Audiology, 6,* 171-177.

Kapteyn, T.S. (1977c). Factors in the appreciation of a prosthetic rehabilitation. *Audiology, 16,* 446-452.

Kopra, L.L., Kopra, M.A., Abrahamson, J.E., and Dunlop, R.J. (1986). Development of sentences graded in difficulty for lipreading practice. *Journal of the Academy of Rehabilitative Audiology, 19,* 71-86.

Kretschmer, R.R. and Kretschmer, L.W. (1978). *Language development and intervention with the hearing impaired.* Baltimore: University Park Press.

Kretschmer, R.R. and Kretschmer, L.W. (1980). Pragmatics: Development in normal-hearing and hearing-impaired children. In Subtelny, J.D. (Ed.), *Speech assessment and speech improvement for the hearing impaired.* Washington, DC: A.G. Bell Association for the Deaf, 268-290.

Kricos, P.B. and Lesner, S.A. (1982). Differences in visual intelligibility across talkers. *Volta Review, 84,* 219-225.

Kushner, H.S. (1981). *When bad things happen to good people.* London: Pan Books.

Kyle, J.G. (1985). Deaf people: Assessing the community or the handicap? *Bulletin of the British Psychological Society, 38,* 137-141.

Kyle, J.G., Jones, L.G., and Wood, P.L. (1985). Adjustment to acquired hearing loss: A working model. In Orlans, H. (Ed.), *Adjustment to adult hearing loss*. San Diego: College-Hill Press, 119-138.

Lesner, S.A., Sandridge, S.A., and Kricos, P.B. (1987). Training influences on visual consonant and sentence recognition. *Ear and Hearing, 8,* 283-287.

Lewis, D. (1978). *The secret language of your child*. London: Souvenir Press.

Lieth, L.v.d. (1972a). Experimental social deafness. *Scandinavian Audiology, 1,* 81-87.

Lieth, L.v.d. (1972b). Hearing tactics. *Scandinavian Audiology, 1,* 155-160.

Ling, D. (1976). *Speech and the hearing-impaired child: Theory and practice*. Washington, DC: A.G. Bell Association for the Deaf.

Ling, D. (Ed.) (1984). *Early intervention for hearing-impaired children: Oral options*. San Diego: College-Hill Press.

Ling, D. and Nienhuys, T.G. (1983). The deaf child: Habilitation with and without a cochlear implant. *Annals of Otology, Rhinology, and Laryngology, 92,* 593-598.

Lipscombe, D.M. (1978). *Noise and audiology*. Baltimore: University Park Press.

Livneh, H. (1982). On the origins of negative attitudes toward people with disabilities. *Rehabilitation Literature, 43,* 338-347.

Lovell, R.B. (1980). *Adult learning*. London: Croon Helm.

Lubinski, R., Duchan, J., and Weitzner-Lin, B. (1980). Analysis of breakdowns and repairs in aphasic adult communication. In Brookshire, R.H. (Ed.), *Clinical Aphasiology Conference Proceedings*. Minneapolis: BRK Publishers, 111-116.

Lubinsky, J. (1983). Training with a vibrotactile aid: A case report. *Journal of the Academy of Rehabilitative Audiology, 16,* 43-48.

Lubinsky, J. (1986). Choosing aural rehabilitation directions: Suggestions from a model of information processing. *Journal of the Academy of Rehabilitative Audiology, 19,* 27-41.

Lundborg, T., Risberg, A., Holmqvist, C., Lindstrom, B., and Svard, I. (1982). Rehabilitative procedures in sensorineural hearing loss. *Scandinavian Audiology, 11,* 161-170.

Luterman, D. (1984). *Counselling the communicatively disordered and their families.* Boston: Little, Brown, and Company.

Lutman, M.E. and Haggard, M.P. (1983). *Hearing science and hearing disorders.* London: Academic Press.

Lyon, M. (1985). The verbal interaction of mothers and their preschool hearing-impaired children. A preliminary investigation. *British Journal of Teachers of the Deaf, 9,* 119-129.

Markides, A. (1977). Rehabilitation of people with acquired deafness in adulthood. *British Journal of Audiology (Supplement 1),* 1-97.

Mason, M.K. (1939). Individual deviations in the visual reproduction of the speech of two speakers. *American Annals of the Deaf, 84,* 408-424.

Maurer, J.F. and Rupp, R.R. (1979). *Hearing and aging.* New York: Grune and Stratton.

McCall, R. (1984). *Speechreading and listening tactics.* London: Robert Hale Limited.

McCarthy, P.A. and Alpiner, J.G. (1982). The remediation process. In Alpiner, J.G. (Ed.), *Handbook of adult rehabilitative audiology (2nd ed.).* Baltimore: Williams and Wilkins, 99-136.

McLaughlin, M.L. (1984). *Conversation: How talk is organized.* Beverley Hills: SAGE Publications.

Meadow-Orlans, K.P. (1985). Social and psychological effects of hearing loss in adulthood: A literature review. In Orlans, H. (Ed.), *Adjustment to adult hearing loss.* San Diego: College-Hill Press, 35-57.

Miller, G.A. and Nicely, P.E. (1955). An analysis of perceptual confusions among some English consonants. *Journal of the Acoustical Society of America, 27,* 338-352.

Miller, G.A., Heise, G.A., and Lichten, W. (1951). The intelligibility of speech as a function of the context of the test materials. *Journal of Experimental Psychology, 41,* 329-335.

Moerk, E.L. (1977). *Pragmatic and semantic aspects of early language development.* Baltimore: University Park Press, 135-146.

Mohay, H. (1986). The adjustment of maternal conversation to hearing and hearing-impaired children: A twin study. *Journal of the British Association of Teachers of the Deaf, 10,* 37-44.

Montgomery, A.A., Walden, B., Schwartz, D., and Prosek, R. (1984). Training auditory visual speech reception in adults with moderate sensorineural hearing loss. *Ear and Hearing, 5,* 30-36.

Morkovin, B.V. (1947). Rehabilitation of the aurally handicapped through the study of speech reading in life situations. *Journal of Speech and Hearing Disorders, 12,* 363-368.

Mulac, A., Danhauer, J.L., and Johnson, C.E. (1983). Young adults' and peers' attitudes toward elderly hearing aid wearers. *Australian Journal of Audiology, 5,* 57-62.

Murray, N. and Byrne, D. (1986). Performance of hearing-impaired and normal hearing listeners with various high frequency cut-offs in hearing aids. *Australian Journal of Audiology, 8,* 21-28.

Nabelek, A.K. and Letowski, R.R. (1985). Vowel confusions of hearing-impaired listeners under reverberent and nonreverberent conditions. *Journal of Speech and Hearing Disorders, 58,* 126-131.

Nabelek, A.K. and Pickett, J.M. (1974). Monaural and binaural speech perception through hearing aids under noise and reverberation with normal and hearing-impaired listeners. *Journal of Speech and Hearing Research, 17,* 724-739.

Newman, C.W. and Weinstein, B.E. (1986). Judgements of perceived hearing handicap by hearing-impaired elderly men and their spouses. *Journal of the Academy of Rehabilitative Audiology, 19,* 109-115.

Nienhuys, T., Cross, T., and Horsborough, K. (1984). Child variables influencing maternal speech style: Deaf and hearing children. *Journal of Communication Disorders, 17,* 184-207.

Oja, G.L. and Schow, R.L. (1984). Hearing aid evaluation based on measures of use and satisfaction. *Ear and Hearing, 5,* 77-85.

Okun, B.F. and Rappaport, L.J. (1980). *Working with families: An introduction to family therapy.* North Scituate, MA: Duxbury Press.

O'Neil, M.R. (Ed.) (1978). *Learning strategies.* New York: Academic Press.

Owens, E. (1983). An overview to cochlear implants in relation to aural rehabilitation and habilitation. *Journal of the Academy of Rehabilitative Audiology, 16,* 68-86.

Owens, E. and Raggio, M. (1987). The UCSF tracking procedure for evaluation and training of speech reception by hearing-impaired adults. *Journal of Speech and Hearing Disorders, 52,* 120-128.

Owens, E. and Telleen, C.C. (1981). Tracking as an aural rehabilitative process. *Journal of the Academy of Rehabilitative Audiology, 14,* 259-272.

Owens, E., Benedict, M., and Schubert, E.D. (1972). Consonant phonemic errors associated with pure-tone configurations and certain kinds of hearing impairment. *Journal of Speech amd Hearing Research, 15,* 308-322.

Parret, H. (1971). *Language and discourse.* Paris: Mouton, 89-90.

Pendleton, D. and Hasler, J. (Eds.) (1983). *Doctor-patient communication.* London: Academic Press.

Pengilley, P. (1977). *By word of mouth (3rd ed.).* Melbourne: Victorian Deaf Society, HEAR Service.

Perls, F.S. (1969). *Gestalt therapy verbatim.* Moab, UT: Real People Press.

Pesonen, J. (1968). Phoneme communication of the deaf. *Annals of the Finnish Academy of Science, 151* (Series B).

Pflaster, G. (1979). Mirror, mirror on the wall .....? *Journal of Speech and Hearing Disorders, 44,* 379-387.

Picheny, M.A., Durlach, N.I., and Braida, L.D. (1985). Speaking clearly for the hard of hearing: Intelligibility differences between clear and conversational speech. *Journal of Speech and Hearing Research, 28,* 96-103.

Picheny, M.A., Durlach, N.I., and Braida, L.D. (1986). Speaking clearly for the hard of hearing II: Acoustic characteristics of clear and conversational speech. *Journal of Speech and Hearing Research, 29,*   434-446.

Pickett, J.M. (1979). On somesthetic transforms of speech for deaf persons. In McPherson, D.L. (Ed.), *Advances in prosthetic devices for the deaf.* Rochester, NY: National Technical Institute for the Deaf, 184-188.

Pickett, J.M., Martin, E.S., Johnson, D., Smith, S.B., Daniel, Z., Willis, D., and Otis, W. (1972). On patterns of speech feature reception by deaf listeners. In Fant, G. (Ed.), *Speech communication ability and profound deafness.* Washington, DC: A.G. Bell Association for the Deaf, 119-133.

Plant, G. (1980). Visual identification of Australian vowels and diphthongs. *Australian Journal of Audiology, 2,* 2-6.

Plant, G.L. and Macrae, J.H. (1981). The NAL lipreading test: Development, standardisation, and validation. *Australian Journal of Audiology, 3,* 49-57.

Plant, G., Macrae, J., Dillon, H., and Pentecost, F. (1984). A single-channel vibrotactile aid to lipreading: Preliminary results with an experienced subject. *Australian Journal of Audiology, 6,* 55-64.

Plomp, R. (1978). Auditory handicap of hearing impairment and the limited benefit of hearing aids. *Journal of the Acoustical Society of America, 63,* 533-549.

Pratt, C. and Nesdale, A.R. (1984). Pragmatic awareness in children. In Tunmer, W.E., Pratt, C., and Herriman, M.L. (Eds.), *Meta-linguistic awareness in children*. Berlin: Springer-Verlag, 105-125.

Prince, G. (1982). Narratology: The form and functioning of narrative. *Janua Linguarum*, Series Major 108. Berlin: Mouton.

Prutting, C.A. and Kirchner, D.M. (1987). A clinical appraisal of the pragmatic aspects of language. *Journal of Speech and Hearing Disorders, 52*, 105-119.

Punch, J.L. and Beck, E.L. (1980). Low-frequency response of hearing aids and judgements of aided speech quality. *Journal of Speech and Hearing Disorders, 45*, 325-335.

Ripich, D.N. and Spinelli, F.M. (1985). An ethnographic approach to assessment and intervention. In Ripich, D.N. and Spinelli, F.M. (Eds.), *School discourse problems*. San Diego: College-Hill Press, 199-217.

Roeser, R.J., Friel-Patti, S., and Henderson, T.S. (1983). Evaluating a tactile aid for the reception of speech. *Journal of the Academy of Rehabilitative Audiology, 16*, 49-67.

Rook, K.S. (1984). Promoting social bonding: Strategies for helping the lonely and socially isolated. *American Psychologist, 39*, 1389-1407.

Rousey, C. (1976). Psychological reactions to hearing loss. *Journal of Speech and Hearing Disorders, 36*, 382-389.

Rubenstein, A. and Boothroyd, A. (1987). Effect of two approaches to auditory training on speech recognition by hearing-impaired adults. *Journal of Speech and Hearing Research, 30*, 153-160.

Sacks, H., Schegloff, E.A., and Jefferson, G.A. (1974). A simplest systematics for the organization of turn-taking for conversation. *Language, 50*, 696-735.

Sanders, D.A. (1982). *Aural rehabilitation (2nd ed.)*. Englewood Cliffs, NJ: Prentice-Hall.

Saywitz, K. and Wilkinson, T.C. (1982). Age-related differences in metalinguistic awareness. In Kuczaj, S.A. (Ed.), *Language development: Vol. 2, Language, thought, and culture.* Hillsdale, NJ: Erlbaum, 229-250.

Schindler, R.A. and Merzenich, M.M. (Eds.) (1985). *Cochlear implants.* New York: Raven Press.

Schlesinger, H.S. (1985). The psychology of hearing loss. In Orlans, H. (Ed.), *Adjustment to adult hearing loss.* San Diego: College-Hill Press, 99-118.

Schuknecht, H.F. (1974). *Pathology of the ear.* Cambridge, MA: Harvard University Press.

Schulte, K. (1978). The use of supplementary speech information in verbal communication. *Volta Review,* 80, 12-20.

Schwartz, J.R. and Black, J.W. (1967). Some effects of sentence structure on speechreading. *Central States Speech Journal,* 18, 86-90.

Sher, A. and Owens, E. (1974). Consonant confusions associated with hearing loss above 2000 Hz. *Journal of Speech and Hearing Research,* 17, 669-681.

Sims, D.G. (1982). Hearing and speechreading evaluation for the deaf adult. In Sims, D.G., Walter, G.G., and Whitehead, R.L. (Eds.), *Deafness and Communication.* Baltimore: Williams and Wilkins, 141-154.

Sims, D.G. (1985). Adults with hearing impairment. In Katz, J. (Ed.), *Handbook of clinical audiology (3rd ed.).* Baltimore: Williams and Wilkins, 1017-1045.

Slater, R. (1987). On helping people with tinnitus to help themselves. *British Journal of Audiology,* 21, 87-90.

Stephens, S.D.G. (1980). Evaluating the problems of the hearing impaired. *Audiology,* 19, 205-220.

Stubbs, M. (1983). *Discourse analysis.* Chicago: University of Chicago Press.

Studebaker, G.A. and Bess, F.H. (Eds.) (1982). *The Vanderbilt hearing aid report.* Upper Darby, PA: Monographs in Contemporary Audiology.

Sumby, W.H. and Pollack, I. (1954). Visual contribution to speech intelligibility in noise. *Journal of the Acoustical Society of America, 26,* 212-215.

Surr, R.K., Schuchman, G.I., and Montgomery, A.A. (1978). Factors influencing use of hearing aids. *Archives of Otolaryngology, 104,* 732-736.

Urbantschitsch, V. (1895). *Auditory training for deaf mutism and acquired deafness.* English translation by Silverman, S.R (1985). Washington, DC: A.G. Bell Association for the Deaf.

Ventry, I.M. and Weinstein, B.E. (1982). The Hearing Handicap Inventory for the Elderly: A new tool. *Ear and Hearing, 3,* 128-134.

Ventry, I.M. and Weinstein, B.E. (1983). Identification of elderly people with hearing problems. *ASHA, 25,* 37-42.

Villchur, E. (1974). Simulation of the effect of recruitment on loudness relationships in speech. *Journal of the Acoustical Society of America, 56,* 1601-1611.

Villchur, E. (1978). Signal processing. In Ross, M. and Giolas, T.G. (Eds.), *Auditory management of hearing-impaired children.* Baltimore: University Park Press, 219-237.

Walden, B.E. and Montgomery, A.A. (1975). Dimensions of consonant perception in normal and hearing-impaired listeners. *Journal of Speech and Hearing Research, 18,* 444-455.

Walden, B.E., Erdman, S.A., Montgomery, A.A., Schwartz, D.M., and Prosek, R.A. (1981). Some effects of training on speech recognition by hearing-impaired adults. *Journal of Speech amd Hearing Research, 24,* 207-216.

Walden, B.E., Montgomery, A.A., Prosek, R.A., and Schwartz, D.M. (1980). Consonant similarity judgements by normal and hearing-impaired listeners. *Journal of Speech and Hearing Research, 23,* 162-184.

Walden, B.E., Prosek, R.A., Montgomery, A.A., Scherr, C.K., and Jones, C.J. (1977). Effects of training on the visual recognition of consonants. *Journal of Speech and Hearing Research, 20,* 130-145.

Watzlawick, P., Bavelas, J.B., and Jackson, D.D. (1967). *Pragmatics of human communication.* New York: Norton.

Webster, E.J. and Newhoff, M. (1981). Intervention with families of communicatively impaired adults. In Beasley, D.S. and Davis, G.A. (Eds.), *Aging: Communication processes and disorders.* New York: Grune and Stratton, 229-240.

Weiner, S. and Goodenough, D. (1977). A move toward a psychology of conversation. In Freedle, R. (Ed.), *Discourse production and comprehension.* Norwood, NJ: Ablex, 213-225.

Weinstein, B.E. and Ventry, I.M. (1983). Audiometric correlates of the Hearing Handicap Inventory for the Elderly. *Journal of Speech and Hearing Disorders, 48,* 379-384.

Weinstein, B.E., Spitzer, J.B., and Ventry, I.M. (1986). Test-retest reliability of the Hearing Handicap Inventory for the Elderly. *Ear and Hearing, 7,* 295-299.

Weisenberger, J.M. and Miller, J.D. (1987). The role of tactile aids in providing information about acoustic stimuli. *Journal of the Acoustical Society of America, 82,* 906-916.

Wiig, E.H. and Semel, E. (1984). *Language assessment and intervention for the learning disabled (2nd ed.).* Columbus, OH: Merrill.

Woodward, H.M.E. (1964). The structural component of linguistic meaning and the reading of normally hearing and deaf children. *Report of the Proceedings of the International Congress on Education of the Deaf and of the Forty-First Meeting of the Convention of American Instructors of the Deaf.* Washington, DC: U.S. Government Printing Office, 536-540.

World Health Organization (1980). *International classification of impairments, disabilities, and handicaps.* Geneva: World Health Organization.

Yalom, I. (1980). *Existential psychotherapy.* New York: Basic Books.

Yorkston, K.M., Beukelman, D.R., and Flowers, C.R. (1980). Efficiency of information exchange between aphasic speakers and communication partners. In Brookshire, R.H. (Ed.), *Clinical Aphasiology Conference Proceedings.* Minneapolis: BRK Publishers, 96-105.

SUBJECT INDEX